Stories of Clean Living, the Dutch-American Way

By
Jenn Miller

Jennerick Press
Fort Wayne, Indiana

Published by Jennerick Press.

For information about this book and other Jennerick Press books please visit us on the web at Jennerick.com or e-mail us at Information@Jennerick.com

ISBN 978-0-9824484-0-3

First Edition: April 2009

Dedicated to Stephanie,
my crazy redhead.

Table of Contents

Calvinettes

We have a word for good girls. When I say "we," I mean my cousin Stephanie and I. To be fair, she used the word first, and I appropriated it. I am not nearly as clever as she is. However, I am the writer, so I get to pretend things are my own original idea just because I write down other people's good ideas faster than they can finish expressing them.

And when I say "good girls," I mean specifically those females whom our people hold up as examples to the world of what it means to be a proper Dutch-American woman of the Reformed tradition: She is an A or B student whose hair (usually blonde) is as obedient as her predestined soul; she seems to wear clothes not only for the purpose of covering her nakedness, but as a demonstration of how well her mother taught her to use an iron; her home has floors, toilet seats and refrigerator tops on which you could hygienically deliver a baby; she is a trusted baby-sitter who grows up into a suitably married mother of at least three scrubbed, matching and quiet children who always occupy one of the front 12 pews in church (but never the very front row, which is for late-comers); she has at least enough education to be able to answer on demand the first question of the Heidelberg Catechism, but she is so kind and pure of heart she may not always be smart enough to understand your sarcasm. If you have seen our college brochures, she is somewhere in those glossy pages. If our people belonged to the kind of mega-church that paid for billboard advertising along the highway – which they emphatically are NOT – this is the woman you would see smiling down at you from above, beckoning to come and discover whatever it is that God has done to put such a beatific smile on her face.

The word we so maliciously attach to this worthy, upstanding and lovely female is "Calvinette."

The term comes from a very real thing. It is a now-unused word for our own Dutch Reformed version of Girl Scouts. Nowadays they call this group GEMS, which stands for "Girls Everywhere Meeting the Savior." Which, as much as this remains a fine and worthy organization with the best of intentions, and with the best of our women running the show, it is a name that somehow makes my broken brain think of a cult of little girls marching off into the sunset to bravely meet their sure demise. "Ready girls? Let's all go meet the Savior!"

I desperately wanted to be in Girl Scouts when I was in the third grade, thanks to a fourth-grade cookie-pusher named Jill who attended my small parochial school in Highland, Indiana. She had gleaming, thick, dark brown braids and bangs so straight you could have used her head as a measuring device for hanging picture frames. My own dull, medium-brown hair was so wispy and fine that my braids lasted barely through recess, and I feared that my bangs were sometimes skewed from being cut while sitting in a wobbly chair in my parents' basement utility room, which had a cement floor slanted toward the central drainpipe.

During Girl Scout Cookie season, Jill would come to school at least once a week in her uniform: an adorable khaki vest, skirt, knee socks and a sash with an astonishing number of badges and pins and colorful doodads all over it. One time, Jill wore a matching beret. That clinched it.

"Mom, I want to be a Girl Scout."

My mother, who is a better Christian than I am, and to whom my cousins all refer with great respect as "Auntie Herbie," looked down from her ironing (Yes, she WAS ironing at the time) and said, "We don't go to Girl Scouts. That's secular." If you had grown up in a house like mine, you would not bat an eye at somebody using the word "secular" to a third grader. So I countered with more logic: "Jill is a Girl Scout, and she's in fourth grade at Highland Christian."

Mom looked at me like I should have known better. "Jill's family is different. They're Presbyterians."

"But I want to go camping and make cookies and stuff."

"We have Calvinettes. Ours is better because it's at church."

Indeed. Better, because it employed that thing which pervaded all aspects of my early education, whether it was Sunday School or my regular school work: Bible verse memorization and recitation. At every meeting of the Calvinettes, we recited a verse together that I have never forgotten. I still hear it in my head to this day, because I believe the verse cuts to the core of everything it means to be a Christian. Even though I have sought much more liberal ground with the Episcopal Church – and, if I am honest, I do so because my friends go there, and nobody gets on my case if I skip church or go to Target on Sunday – I still remember fondly this part of growing up Christian Reformed, and I still place a great deal of value on memorization, a skill that is now completely lost in the education system, both public and private.

Each meeting of the Calvinettes would begin with our director, Eileen, an angelic grown-up Calvinette who served for about 85 years, and never appeared to age a single day (a phenomenon I apply to the fact that she never had a negative word to say about anybody), asking us, "Calvinettes, what does the Lord require of you?"

In Rotarian predictability, our reply was always, wherever in the world Calvinettes might be meeting: "To do justice, to love kindness, and to walk humbly with our God." I can still hear the select few over-achievers tacking on to the end, "Micah 6:8," like an aural bibliography. Also, I can still see the large blue poster board with the verse handwritten in marker, which nobody but the fourth-graders needed. I would be surprised to meet any Calvinette on the street who could not recite that question and answer. Indeed, I would be very surprised just to meet another Calvinette on the street anywhere, except for maybe in my home of Northwest Indiana, or in rural Iowa or Minnesota, or in our people's Mecca of Grand Rapids, Michigan.

The next year, I and my fellow fourth graders at Second Highland Christian Reformed Church, not incidentally located adjacent to our school, put on the required breastplate of righteousness every second and fourth Wednesday of the month: navy blue slacks, a button-down white shirt and a white kerchief with blue stitch trim – a blank snowy field upon which all of our mothers' future hopes and dreams for their gifted young girls would play out over the next five years. The kerchief was fastened in the front with a leather slide, dyed navy blue with a white silhouette of a young, pert-nosed girl with a paige-boy haircut, solemnly placing her palms together in an ironically Catholic sort of prayer-pose (our people pray strictly with hands folded, fingers entwined).

My white kerchief remained generally clutter-free in terms of badges throughout my Calvinette career. That is not to say I failed. I earned exactly the required number of badges each year. I surmounted tasks involving baby-sitting, baking, camping, latch-hooking and some sort of Bible verse memorization. Enough to get by. Enough so that people other than my mother would not hassle me about it. Though I do not know what would have happened if I failed to earn the minimum number of badges each year. It is not as if they could have kicked me out of Calvinettes. How can you kick someone out who is predestined to be there?

You could not. Because the goal was not to get good grades in the form of tiny square badges with pictures of blue, puffy stick figures celebrating their achievements in vegetable gardening. Or even to make Christmas angels out of folded pieces of satin and lace, a particularly difficult craft that had me crying, and had the ever merciful Eileen finishing my project for me out of pity.

The goal of Calvinettes was to guide us into becoming ladies, in preparation for the eighth-grade level — that longed-for year when we Calvinettes tore off our white be-dazzled kerchiefs and wore blue jeans and dress shirts to Calvinette meetings. For that was when they put us in "Charm Course." Until that much-anticipated year, we were all expected to aim for the highest honor of all. The Gold Star, which would be handed, ceremoniously at the annual Mother/Daughter Banquet, to the Calvinette who earned the highest number of badges. The girl who cooked, cleaned, babysat, memorized, baked, latch-hooked, cross-stitched, sewed, prayed, photographed, camped, and decorated herself into a frenzied streak of navy blue and white.

You would think they could come up with a better, more original award than a Gold Star. I mean, what were we thinking, handing out mystical five-pointed star badges to little Christian girls? This was not the Masonic Lodge, after all. And our people most certainly did NOT approve of anything Masonic, or any secretive fraternal organization that encouraged its male members to wear aprons and use charity as an excuse to make a nuisance of themselves at parades with their tiny motorized cars. I think for us girls, a better symbol of our ultimate achievement would be a gold wooden shoe.

There was no point in me aiming for the Gold Star. Not with a classmate like my friend Michelle, who snagged that honor at least three times in the five years we slogged through Calvinettes. For she was the iconic Calvinette. She was beautiful, athletic, mature, responsible, intelligent, well-spoken, polite, participatory, fun, a great clarinet player and above all, nice. So nice, there was not a single person in our class who could not call her a friend. I wanted to hate her but I could not. I really, really liked being around Michelle. And of course, my mother liked me being around Michelle because she hoped, no doubt, that some of Michelle's Lisa Simpson tendencies would rub off. Unfortunately the only Lisa Simpson attribute I ever exhibited had little to do with grades or musical proficiency, and more to do with questioning the decisions of adults, namely why they insisted on sheltering their girls and boys so thoroughly that they could not even participate in Scouts without fear of appearing ungodly, or worse, Presbyterian.

With Michelle, the Gold Star ringer on my team, I figured there was no point in trying to steal her thunder. She was such a good person, who would want to? So instead of trying to earn more badges than she did, my occasional visits to Michelle's household in those days consisted mostly of playing Barbies, which I happily discovered she enjoyed doing as much as I did. She, too, liked to make Ken kiss Malibu Barbie, prompting elaborate cat fights between the tan-lined doll and the satin-wrapped Beauty Secrets Barbie. The rest of my time at her house was spent making and eating the fluffiest and yummiest cinnamon rolls east of the Mississippi.

Michelle's mother was a thin, fastidious woman who was not of Dutch descent – as are the larger, lumpier women in my family – and yet she knew how to bake the delicious things that made the rest of us large and lumpy.

Michelle never gained weight from all those years of baking at the side of her mother. I envisioned her father driving her straight to the gym after every cinnamon bun she ate. One of my summer afternoons with Michelle did in fact involve a trip to a popular local work-out facility on 45th Street in Highland, called Sports Illustrated, of all things. Because I am nothing if not a distraction for other people from their hard work, Michelle and I walked the track a few times, chit-chatting the whole way. Her father, a rowing-machine enthusiast, was not impressed with the lack of sweat we had produced at the end of our session. We were in fifth grade at the time; I still do not know what was wrong with that man.

I had tried explaining to my mother about Michelle's family's freakish perfection year after year, but it was no good. Every spring Mom and I would go shopping for dresses to wear to the banquet. Every year we'd be seated next to each other on metal folding chairs in our church's basement that smelled of Crayola and diapers. We'd sit there drinking store-bought, tepid lemonade and enjoying an entire meal served by apron-wearing dads – an annual performance that you'd think was on the level of a drag show with all the *sturm und drang* that would precede it. And every year, after the dinner, all the young and old ladies would hoof it up the stairs into the sanctuary, where our fearless leader Eileen and all the counselors, ersatz troop leaders, would perform something that amounted to a variety show for the mothers. Skits were performed, solos sung and pianos played, but this was all a pale precursor to the real reason we were all there. After all that nonsense, Eileen would finally announce the winner of the Gold Star. And every year, the winner was not me.

And every year, my poor, long-suffering mother would clap and smile as graciously and sincerely as Susan Lucci at the Daytime Emmys, while, quietly, her dim hope was snuffed out that somehow I had decided to buckle down and churn out fifty badges as a surprise ending for her. Alas, I would continue to disappoint my saintly mother for the next two decades. If it was not Calvinettes, I was a sad sack at flute playing, softball throwing, house cleaning and catechism memorization.

Later on, as Michelle and I journeyed through junior high together, the differences between her family and my family started to take shape. My grandfather had hand-built a wet bar in the finished basement at the house where I grew up. When I was in seventh grade, I found out through a mutual friend that Michelle's parents were no longer allowing her to come to my slumber parties, specifically because they had found out about the wet bar. Not that it was ever a secret. And never mind that the only thing behind that bar was an empty mini-fridge, several shelves of glass barware in the Tiara pine cone pattern and a 12-year-old bottle of blueberry schnapps. The only danger that awaited young girls at Bill and Herbie's basement might be a wall-shaking freight train passing by, resulting in an avalanche of bowling trophies and a mounted walleye fish. No pre-teen girls were injured during their overnight stays in the basement, and neither did anybody have any interest in cracking open the blueberry schnapps.

But that is why Michelle always won the Gold Star. She was a true Calvinette, born from a true Calvinette mother. Irreproachable, incorruptible, and focused on the prize.

Once we hit eighth grade, we were no longer Calvinettes, but members of Charm Course. No longer did we do badges or wear the white kerchiefs. This was a sort of vague stage where the organization was supposed to prepare us for high school. Michelle did not need Charm Course. She was the definition of charm. Really, I think they should have found a special provision in the Calvinette by-laws to just let the girl graduate early, but I am sure they just kept her around as an example to the rest of us. What troop leader would not want a girl like her in their social/religious/civic club? She ups the counselor success quotient by at least 85,000 points.

I have no freaking clue what charms I was supposed to have learned that eighth-grade year of Calvinettes. But I do vividly remember listening to several instructional talks from our counselors about how to keep horny Dutch boys from getting into our pants. Those well-meaning ladies should be comforted to know their lessons on sex did get through to me, and stuck with me throughout my teen-age years. The only boys who ever made it past second base with me were German Lutherans.

I so wish we Calvinettes had spent less time guarding ourselves against peer pressure and more time actually camping, like the Girl Scouts we all pretended to be. I love to camp, and I love all levels of camping, from spartan style tenting, all the way up to the Episcopalian version of camping, which involves staying in furnished WPA cabins at state parks, where the rangers bring you fresh towels every day.

For some reason, I only recall one camping trip we took as Calvinettes, to Camp Tecumseh. Likely, our group did in fact attend every year, and I just did not go because I had failed to ask my mom and dad fill out the proper paperwork in a timely fashion. This usually explained my lack of attendance at many things. On another occasion, I horrified my mother by missing out on my fourth-grade teacher's wedding, to which our entire class had been invited. I had simply forgotten to mention it to my mom when I first received the invitation, and then on every passing day, I became more and more scared that I would get yelled at for failing to mention it. So, like most of my personal problems, I pretended to forget about it and hoped that it would go away and my slacking would be overlooked.

Whatever was going on in my mind at any given time was always more important than the reality, and the reality is that my upstanding parents desperately wanted me to fit in and be a participant. And so, eventually, I ended up at a weekend camp out at Tecumseh.

There was bad mojo all around this camp out. I have not a single fond memory of it. First, the bathhouses were not very clean, and as a result one of my fellow Calvinettes refused to go number two for the entire weekend. The only reason I know this is because she made a pronouncement of it, to everyone's astonishment. I actually think she was lying about that, and just enjoying the attention and sympathy, and possibly the indirect admiration for her mother, who must have been so good a housewife that her own daughter could not bear to perform a necessary bodily function on a less-than gleaming toilet.

One of my other dim memories of this trip was my period scare. At one point, a group of us were hiking in the woods on the way to the pool. I was wearing only my bathing suit and carrying a towel. We were escorted by a swarm of bugs. Some alert Calvinette pointed at my crotch and said, "You have your period!" I did indeed feel some moisture down in that region. I looked down, and hello neighbor! There was blood.

But the blood did not make sense. A closer inspection by me revealed the blood was not coming from the nether regions, but there was just a certain amount of blood between my thighs. Ever since the sixth grade, I was an overweight kid. At that age, I would not say I was fat by my own standards, but I was a chunky girl with chubby, pre-pubescent thighs that rubbed together when I walked. Apparently an ill-fated mosquito had chosen this plump area on which to land, unbeknownst to me, and had suffered death by chubster friction. And now the blood that was inside the mosquito was on the insides of my legs. One counselor came up to me, placed her hand on my shoulder, and asked, "Honey, do you need a Tampax?" I said, no, it was a mosquito bite. The woman looked at my sympathetically, as if she knew and I knew that I was lying, but she was going to be my special confidant and keep my secret. I wondered if everyone around me was just plain stupid. Had none of these woman ever been caught by surprise by a menstrual flow? Because those kinds of surprises certainly do not look like this.

And anyway, I could not fathom using a tampon of any kind at the time. The first time I did get my period, I had been holed up in a campground bathroom stall at Jellystone Park, crying over the tiny, shocking illustrations that came with the box of Tampax. My mother, a Stayfree maxi-pad loyalist, had given up trying to explain the mechanics of tampon insertion and just said, "If you wanna go on the waterslide, you gotta use a cork. Me, I just don't swim when I'm on the rag." For all her saintliness, my mother runs a bit salty at times.

As it happened, I was not on my period at Camp Tecumseh. All was right with me. But other bathroom issues raged on. The last morning of the trip, all 200 girls and counselors representing the entire northern Indiana region of

Calvinettes gathered in the meeting hall for a final worship service. The outfit certainly could not send us on our way on a Sunday morning without a proper hour of church. What made this particular service so special was not only did we receive a royal reaming out by one of our leaders, but we got to hear a vulgarity. Over a loudspeaker. From a Calvinette counselor.

It happened when one of our Highland women, Mrs. Z, approached the microphone for some "housekeeping" items about packing up procedures. Then suddenly the tone changed. She paused, mid-sentence, and looked down at her chest, biting back either anger or tears or both. She continued: "Girls, I'm sad to tell you this morning that I'm very disappointed in you. The park ranger came to me this morning, and he asked me to come with him to one of our bathrooms. He said one of our girls had apparently vandalized the stall. I looked inside, and there was POOP! On the toilet seat!" She blurted the word "poop" in a frightening, high-pitched exclamation that was hilarious and embarrassing at the same time, like watching a grown adult imitate a choo-choo train. The tears were beginning to well up, and she repeated the phrase, like she had to say it out loud a second time because she could hardly believe her own ears the first time.

"Poop! On the toilet seat! And I ... had to clean it up."

She concluded by asking anyone who might know who committed this crime to please come forward with the information. The good girls, the real Calvinettes, were of course sitting pale-faced in stunned silence. Other girls were shuddering and red-faced, silently laughing into their fists, which Mrs. Z. likely misconstrued as guilt rather than the fact that she had just performed an unintentional comedy routine for them. As for me, I wondered why she had to be the one to clean up the mess. Didn't they have people there at the camp who cleaned up that kind of thing? Surely this was not the first time someone had missed the target. Typical of me to assume there had to be a system in place to take care of mishaps, well out of the view of my scrubbed and sanitized existence. I suspected at the time that Mrs. Z. cleaned up the mess partially out of shame at the example her Christian girls had set for the secular people working at the camp, and in part out of martyrdom.

I wondered what girl I knew would stoop that low for a prank? We are clean people, and we have a word for things like poop, dirt, dead bugs, and general squalor. This word is "*vies*," pronounced "feece," which in Dutch simply means dirty. But to my people, It implies the deepest dimension of disgustingness, and none of us ever wanted to be caught being *vies*, lest we be labeled *vies*, causing others to stumble into "*viesness*." Spreading poop on a toilet seat was impossibly vies for any of us girls, whose mothers used to scrub the backs of our ears raw during Saturday night baths before sitting us down in front of "Donny and Marie" so they could peacefully set our 5-year-old heads into bristled hair curlers.

I do not think Mrs. Z. ever found out whose poop it was or who did the spreading. And I am glad for it. Because shortly after that speech, word got out on the culprit. The rumor among the Calvinettes was, it was a girl none of us Highlanders knew, thankfully. She was a girl from another church, a girl with a disability, who had most likely had an accident in the bathroom, and was too embarrassed to get help. As far as I can recall, nobody named her name, and nobody pointed her out as the doer of the deed. Those who knew the truth did not see any need in pointing it out, and ended up kindly protecting her from the injustice of public disgrace.

So I guess there was a point to the entire mission of Calvinettes, because by keeping that girl's secret on that day, most of us did exactly what the Lord required of us.

Never Build on Sunday

"Hello?"

"Hi, you are not going to believe this, but Miss Piggy is on Martha Stewart Living and they are making gingerbread houses."

"We need to tape this."

"Done."

Within hours, Stephanie and I are at Strack & Van Til buying up the entire candy aisle. Because, let's face it, that is the real reason anybody would want to build a house out of gingerbread. As we discovered, the candy shopping would turn out to be the most fun part of our lost weekend, which will forever go down in history as the day the Mesman girls called down a bird-poop curse to befall any future gingerbread houses made by Martha Stewart.

Strack & Van Til may be the most familiar grocery store to me, but only because my mother is its most valued customer. She had not yet obtained a drivers license while I was in high school, and would wake me at 6 a.m. every Saturday following my 16th birthday to drive her to the store. By default, therefore, I might be the store's second-most valued customer. A Northwest Indiana chain, Strack & Van Til has a long and legendary history among our people, as many members of the Van Til family have and still do attend my parents' church. All the checkers at the Griffith store knew both my grandmother and my mother.

Years later, when my parents would move to the New Dutch Ghetto of Saint John in 2005, I warned my mother that she was letting down the Van Til clan, as it would be a 30 minute drive to their nearest store, prompting her to find another grocer to fill her daily quota of diet drinks and raisin bread. Mom poo-pooed that notion, but only because she has shaman-like powers. I know this because two weeks after my parents' house in Saint John was finished, so was the shiny new Saint John Strack & Van Til store. Either the Van Til clan got wind that the Dyke family was migrating south, and decided to build there just to keep the annual Herbie revenues rolling in, or my mother requested it. Either way, her level of power is unsettling.

On this day in 1995, my cousins and I are set on building a house of a very different kind. We should have known better. But we have never been the types to think these things through to their conclusions.

The Christmas prior to this one, Stephanie and I had decided we wanted to make our own candles. This was before the prevalence of a Hobby Lobby and Michael's on every corner. We had to drive 30 minutes to the nearest Ben Franklin, because this was the best place for crafts in the area. Now that I am going on 36 and have been a hapless crafter for about 20 years, I prefer supporting local mom-and-pop operations to the big box stores. (In the world of knitting, for example, the best wool and the best advice always comes from your local yarn store.)

The candle project had been doomed from the moment we found our hideously expensive blocks of paraffin wax, putting us way over budget, and we had not even bought the jars, wicks, color, scent or anything else. We had to trim back our grandiose plans, and chose color over scent, for some odd reason. On our way home, both of us twitchy from the amount of money we'd just spent, we tried to convince each other that this was going to turn out great, neither one of us brave enough to say out loud what we knew the other was thinking.

As we made our way back to my home in Griffith, something truly bizarre caught our attention. Ahead of us in the next lane was a shiny black Lincoln Town Car with a license plate that read, "YBPOOR."

I peered over the steering wheel of my 1989 Pontiac Sunbird. "Does that say what I think it says?"

Stephanie looked over. "Y ... B ... POOR." She gasped. "'Why be poor?'! What kind of a jerk gets a license plate like that?"

"That's what I was wondering."

"Why be poor, indeed."

"Mmm-hmmm."

"I can't even believe that."

"I know."

We both shook our heads as we made our way down Ridge Road, still driving behind the Town Car. I decided to escalate it. "You know what we should do?"

"What?" Stephanie was game. Her eyes got big, like she was not sure if she was going to like what I was going to say, but I could still tell she was going to go along with it.

"We should pass him and give him the finger."

We should."

"OK, then."

We did, with me adding a little honk for effect, just in case the elegant silver-haired man in the suit had not noticed the two hysterical young ladies in the car passing him and maniacally laughing while holding up their middle fingers in his direction. I soon realized I was going to have to disappear for good if this was not going to get totally awkward. Who knows how far Mr. YBPOOR was going? We could end up at half a dozen stoplights, idling next to him, and worst of all, him not knowing why we had taken offense at him. So I sped away, probably too fast, and we lost him.

After a few minutes, we had calmed down and I said, "You know, I really hope we read that right."

"I know, I was thinking that, too."

"And, like, maybe it wasn't even his car."

"Oh no!"

"Yeah, we probably should not have done that."

"You're probably right. It probably didn't actually say YBPOOR. It probably said something else."

"Or maybe it meant something else entirely. Like maybe he works with the poor, and dedicates his entire existence to eradicating poverty."

"In a Town Car?"

I thought about this. "You're right. No, he's definitely a jerk."

"I hope so."

Whatever was the case, and whatever that man's intentions were with driving a car with such a bizarre license plate, it put a curse on us. The rest of the afternoon commenced with Stephanie and I taking over my nervous mother's entire windmill-bedecked kitchen: newspapers were spread over every flat surface, and still we managed to sink melted paraffin into the cracks in the table and on the butcher block counter; dozens of pots were coated with melted wax in our trial-and-error method of candle making. We ended up using jelly jars and long-dormant amber-colored Tiara ashtrays for our candles (my parents had quit smoking about ten years prior, but still had a collection of fancy cut-glass ashtrays), with the blue dye we added only lending an anemic baby blue color. I doubt we thought about acquiring an instruction book. In the end, we spent more of our day scraping up bits of wax off my mother's pots and counters, with only a handful of sad looking candles with too-long wicks that did not even smell good when they burned.

Whatever possessed us to proceed with reckless abandon into the gingerbread-house making adventure on that Saturday the following year, I do not know. No, I do know. I blame Martha. This is what Stephanie and I always do when we fail miserably at our attempts to channel our inner domestic divas. We blame Martha and all her complicated steps that take five minutes to complete on the show, when in actuality, each of the individual steps for each of her projects – steps that are completed by her minions, like, days prior to the taping of the witty banter between Martha and Miss Piggy – themselves take at least an hour. Or, in many cases, I suspect, days. If we had considered this fact when we were playing, stopping and rewinding the VCR in my parents' basement that day, we would have run out of steam right then and there, or we would have at least put it off for another week.

Instead, we barreled on through into Sunday. Among the casualties this time was a long list of rules that our people tend to abide by. We spent 10 hours on a Sunday, baking and crafting with Stephanie's sister Kim and our cousin Heather. This is equal to work, which we are not allowed to do on the Lord's Day. We skipped evening church. We ran to the store for forgotten items, thereby causing the heathens to work. And Rule Number Four: "Thou shalt not exhaustedly fashion any graven image, specifically a depiction of the word 'SHIT,' out of gingerbread dough; furthermore, thou shalt not bake the 'shit' and then photograph thyself flaunting such a pastry abomination." This one is a little more obscure than the others, but I am sure it is engraved on a stone tablet somewhere.

Our first mistake was not preparing the gingerbread walls and roofs the day before our Sunday assembly party. Our second mistake was not keeping our misery to ourselves, but instead placing many a stumbling block of sin in front of Kim and Heather.

It all started out innocently enough. Heather and Stephanie and Kim came over to Auntie Herbie's kitchen right after church Sunday morning, and we set about mixing the dough. I do not recall if Heather and Kim were fazed by the fact that we had not thought to make dough ahead of time; I was too excited to see the end result of my candy-coated construction.

We had a lot of work ahead of us, so we decided to get the most done in the least amount of time. Grasping my mother's avocado green hand mixer that she had received as a shower gift more than 20 years earlier, we got to mixing. One thing about gingerbread dough, it is thick. So thick, that it is perhaps unwise to make four batches at once, and certainly unwise to mix even one batch of it with a hand mixer instead of a stand mixer. I blocked out this next part, but my mother tells me that she started smelling that special aroma of the Burning Kitchen Appliance, electricity and grinding metal. And then the smoke started coming out of the thing.

"I think you airheads made four batches of dough in one bowl. You don't do that. And then you tried to mix it with my hand mixer," Mom recalls. "In a way I was kind of glad because I hated that sucker. The beaters would always fall out. And the cord would fall out, too."

Mom explains that she had not previously ditched the old green mixer because in her day, people hung on to things. "You didn't run out and buy a hand mixer. Today, none of that stuff lasts. It's a disposable generation now; they don't make stuff to last anymore."

So I guess our disposable generation thoroughly disposed of my mom's old things in short order. Cousin Heather tells me that I made her go next door and ask to borrow a neighbor's mixer. I certainly do not intentionally block out the more awkward or mean things that I do on a regular basis, so I have no idea why this part does not stick in my memory, though I do apologize to Heather for forcing her to be the one to approach a neighbor whom I barely had the gumption to speak to most of the time I was growing up.

Anyway, I could hardly think about the feelings of others, what with the heavenly aroma that eventually took over the kitchen. It just made me more heady with Stewart/Piggy-inspired crafting glee.

The time it took for the four of us to prepare and bake enough gingerbread for four complete houses ran us well into late afternoon. My mom had only one oven, after all, with three racks, and our house panels were quite large, so we were only able to bake enough panels for about one house at a time. "Shit," we all said at this realization. At about 3:45 p.m., we realized that the actual fun part of our project – the candy part – was hours away.

But this was not the biggest problem. "Shit. We're going to miss church."

Sunday evening church among the Dutch Calvinists takes great priority over baking, crafting, and visiting, but how much priority varies from family to family. My parents were not thrilled, but mostly OK with me skipping out that night. They, too, tended to skip from time to time, especially if Mom did not have to sing in choir, and even more especially when there was a visiting pastor. Or worse, a visiting missionary bringing his annual message in exchange for some much deserved dough. Heather's parents, which included my mom's sister, Bev Z., also did not seem to mind so much as Heather was generally a good kid. Stephanie, whose mother is Bev M. (sister of my dad), pretty much did whatever she wanted and argued about it later with her parents.

Steph's sister, Kim, was a much more compliant child than Stephanie, and was coveted by parents of less-than-stellar children far and wide. So, Aunt Bev M. was, to say the least, not pleased that I was holding her daughter hostage for the evening. A few phone calls were made, parents were placated as best as they could be, and we soldiered on.

Kim was ever-patient with us, but her frustration was becoming evident. "Did you two even think of baking all this shit yesterday?"

Stephanie and I looked at each other. We realized neither of us had even remotely considered that possibility.

"Shit," I said. "That would have been a good idea."

"No," said Steph. "That would make this a two-day project and I would have been bored already."

I considered this. Hmm. "That's true, I would have given up by now."

Kim and Heather, who would both grow up to become teachers, both looked at us as if they were watching a passenger train wreck in slow motion. So completely punchy by that time, Stephanie and I both busted up at the notion that the whole world seemed so incredulous at our lack of planning.

Many years later, Stephanie and I would often wonder why certain people whom we knew did not seem to like us very much. Not so much Kim and Heather, who, despite their exasperation, still "got" us. No, we would often talk about strange looks and odd comments from certain members of our large extended family, or certain grumpy people from church or school. During one of these discussions, I shrugged the whole thing off with "Well, I don't see what the problem is. I happen to think we are delightful." This made Stephanie laugh, and it was my favorite kind of laugh that she would give me from time to time. Sort of an exploding single guffaw, like I had snuck up behind her with my comedy schtick. She agreed. "Yes, we ARE delightful."

At one point during Gingerbread Day, everything came to a screeching halt. All of the panels were baked and we were just waiting for them to cool so we could glue them together with melted sugar, following Martha's recipe. Because we'd made the panels so large, this also meant a longer cooling time. We waited, tested, and waited some more. We were tired, hungry, thirsty and covered in flour and nauseated from the smell of molasses and ginger and spice. If we'd all been in our 20s at this time, I could have easily cranked up the party atmosphere with some hooch, but alas, at least two or more of us were still underage, and Kim was already in enough trouble as it was. Also sad: we had about two cups of dough leftover from making our panel cut-outs.

We did with the dough the only thing we could do. We applied it to our word of the day. About an hour later, after our panels had cooled enough to paste the walls together, out of the oven came the final creation of the day, and I am proud to say we even posed for pictures with our "SHIT"-shaped gingerbread cookies. No, not turds, the actual word "Shit." Twice. My mother, who'd been checking on us from time to time, pretended to be horrified, but I could tell she was highly amused. My mother had to put a great deal of energy into maintaining the propriety of a Calvinette.

And then, as we proceeded to decorate our houses, the shit truly hit the fan. Our wobbly walls and roofs refused to cooperate without enormous amounts of melted sugar, which, in the construction world, would have been a house held together by paint. We declared our decorations to look like shit. The candy we bought was stale and now tasted like shit. And, shit, we'd spent the whole day building up to this, and it was all complete shit. And we'd missed church and now it was way past supper time and, sure as shit, the Bevs were unhappy. We ate our baked cookie "shits" and laughed about our clever abilities to understand a metaphor.

Finally, we grouped our sad little village onto my mother's butcher block counter, unceremoniously took a snapshot, and cursed ourselves and that horrible Stewart woman as we cleaned up my mother's kitchen. Not knowing the first thing about gingerbread house preservation, nobody had thought about putting these monstrosities into the fridge or freezer. Not that they would have fit, but still. I do not know how the other girls' houses faired the next day, but my mother phoned me at work less than 12 hours later to give me the bad news.

I have often attributed my sense of humor to my dad, but here, I have to give my Mom the credit. I was always, forever grateful to take a break from my wretched ironing-of-tuxedo-shirts job to take a phone call. Mom was calling to tell me my roof had caved in. Sadly, I did not even have the consolation of knowing that I could eat the house now, because I already knew it tasted like shit.

"I'm sorry, sweetheart, but your little HUD house has been condemned."

Pudgie Pies and Tornadoes

I was crouched into a ball, my knees tight to my chest as I tried to silence my fearful breathing. I clutched my red plastic flashlight, and checked to make sure it was in the "off" position. The blackness was my blanket. The splintering wood hovel was my cave. If only I could stop shaking and keep perfectly still, lest I clatter the stones I sat on and give away my location. My eyes squeezed tight in the hope that it would not come, or that it would come, and just get it over with already.

If only it would get someone else first. I waited and hoped for the scream, just so I could exhale and maybe utter a perverse scream along with the newest victim. The fright and the joy of it was always a welcome release, followed by the wonder. Which one of us had been caught? Or had she fled in time to get away? Was everybody else still in hiding or was the whole place now a free-for-all?

The suspense was maddening. The thrill of being out after dark at my age, with no firelight to aid the parents' watchful eyes. Never mind that the grown-ups and the campers were nestled in the trees only 50 yards away. The two-story jungle gym of untreated wood, rope ladders, quaky bridges and its endless array of hidey-holes made us a colony of smelly, sweaty ragamuffins roaming from campground to campground, independent of our parents, and our nightly games of flashlight tag made that fantasy of mine come to life a little bit. In minutes, our parents would have us bathed clean in the communal cinder-block showers with its spidery corners and blinking fluorescent lights, then warmed up by the fire and trundled off to bed on canvas-covered foam pads that passed as mattresses in our dutiful Colemans and Starcrafts.

But for as long as the game of flashlight tag lasted, we were children in darkness and in glee. It was all I could do to keep from shrieking with laughter to break the tension and rend the silence. My love of all things Hitchcock started here. My fascination with the dark side began in this little nook, wood slivers and all.

Then I saw my shadow on the pebbles. A light source from somewhere had caught me. Shit. I could not see his face but his flashlight glared down at me like a cop questioning a drug mule on the interstate at midnight. Blind with fear and exhilaration, and also blinded by cousin Denny's flashlight, I scrabbled from out of my cubby hole and flicked on my light, just in time for his grubby little hands to click off his light, and tag me before I could flee to home base at the swing set. I was now IT. Shit again. I flashed the light around and ran in a random direction, hoping to collide with him, or anybody, so I would not have to be IT in the next round. All around me, kids were running and laughing and screaming, and I cursed my feet. Denny was counting to ten. I cried out in frustration that I was such a slow runner, and that my cousins were so merciless as to run around me in the darkness, with no points of light to guide me. Time was up. I was IT. Which meant I was going to be IT indefinitely, because even if I did catch someone with my flashlight in the next round, there was never a time when I could move fast enough to tag them before they sprinted to home base. Even if I could accomplish that feat, I would never escape from being tagged right back in the next second. The boys were alternately beefy and wiry, all whip fast. My legs were long, but my lack of speed and coordination betrayed me on the ball field as well as the playground.

Still, losing at flashlight tag to my cousins was preferable to being The Loser in gym class, in broad daylight. At Highland Christian School, I was the slightly overweight klutz who walked a little funny. On vacation, I was just another kid in pigtails who spent all day in a damp swimsuit with varying amounts of beach grit in her butt crack, who refused to come out of the lake until her lips were blue and shivering, and her sun baked Fonzie beach towel was just the right temperature to absorb the chill. The only differences among us Mesmans were our beach towels. Other cousins had ones with cartoons and superheroes; Stephanie's was her dad's Budweiser towel, which matched Uncle Wes's Budweiser swim trunks and camping string lights.

It was getting late, and I was getting tired of running around after dark, unable to catch any one of my wily cousins. Before we hit the showers, the parents promised a treat of pudgie pies at the fire, and I was famished. I scooted up next to my mom in my woven plastic and aluminum lawn chair. She was already buttering the outsides of my white bread and placing them in the cast iron sandwich maker. "Cherry pie or pizza fillings?" she offered.

"Peanut butter and banana?" She rolled her eyes.

"We don't have any bananas."

I sighed. "Okay, cherry."

"Fine."

"With marshmallow!"

She sighed and shook her head, but went on to spoon the cherry pie goop on one side of the sandwich, and one marshmallow on the other before clasping the iron sides together and handing it off to my dad to place it in the fire. Dad chose a hot orange spot at the base of the fire, a little teepee of heat beneath the burning wood, where the pudgie pie sandwiches cooked most evenly. This was the blessing of my childhood. Mom took care of me and Dad always knew exactly what to do. The next afternoon I learned that there were things outside of my parents' control. My dad was not the strongest man in the world, and did not always know what to do, and my mom was not always completely sure how to take care of me.

There was a forecast of thunderstorms all day on the little portable radio my Mom had brought with us, but it looked like that would be wrong, so we kids played at the beach all day until the purple clouds started to gather.

Just as the lifeguard began calling us all in, we spotted Uncle Wes's bright blue pickup truck pulling into the parking lot as close to the beach as possible. He had the loudest voice of all the Mesmans. And he had the roomiest pickup with a cap on the back, and seats with a table he'd built inside, and therefore the safest thing for hauling a load of wet children.

We piled in, some of us still dripping. I sat on the open tailgate squished among four or five other cousins who'd fought their way to this coveted spot. The tailgate was always the prime location for campground travel. I hung my peach-fuzzy legs over the edge and swung them, my feet still several feet from the ground, and watch the blur of stones and asphalt cracks zoom past my plastic flip-flops. I wished for Uncle Wes to drive fast enough to allow a current of air to tear my flip-flops right off my feet, just for the drama of it. I wished for this every time we rode like this in the open air to the beach, or to the pool, or to the ice cream parlor with the graffiti on the walls and the pool tables and juke box dominated by strange teen-age boys with feathered hair and an affinity for some extremely weird song called "Tom Sawyer."

I thought it would be hilarious if I were to lose my flip-flops; I would walk around the ice cream parlor barefoot and study the 45s on the jukebox, and the teen-age boys would notice I was barefoot and think I was a runaway and therefore an incredibly cool chick who was into music, and then maybe they'd feel sorry for me and give me a quarter so I could play The Beach Boys, and pretend I was from California, which is, of course, the only thing that could make a barefoot, pre-teen runaway even cooler.

With the dark clouds overhead and the creepy stillness in the air, I knew as well as I knew my swimsuit was soaking through my cut-offs that we were not going to the ice cream parlor tonight, and we really were not going to be playing flashlight tag later. The best I could hope for was that somebody had remembered to shelter the wood pile from the coming rain, so we could at least have a campfire once the storm was over. Turns out I should have been praying for the prevention of a natural disaster instead of asking God to save pudgie pie hour. As soon as we were unloaded at the campsite, each set of parents began herding their respective kids inside the campers. The only person not panicking was Uncle Bill K., who stood shirtless in his cutoffs, watching the buzz of activity and smirking at the everybody's edginess. He took a sip of his Stroh's, looked up at the rapidly moving bruise of clouds and said, "It's gonna blow over." His dog, a floppy white mutt named Snoopy, meanwhile, was racing mad circles around him, stopping every few seconds to manically tear up patches of grass. I would learn later, from National Geographic, that many animals act strange right before earthquakes, hurricanes, tsunamis, and tornadoes. Snoopy knew something was up, and so did my mother.

"Sure, Bill," she said. "That's why it's turning green out here."

I had learned first hand that my mom was either a prophet or a witch doctor who could put curses on people. When I was a small child in the 1970s, we'd seen some construction workers building a house on Kleinman Road in Highland. We'd driven by the house on the way to Grandma and Grandpa's house for coffee after church. Mom was upset because there were men working on Sunday, the Lord's Day. "That house is going to fall down." The next week, that house was rubble. I am sure there was a logical explanation, such as poor workmanship. But as a five-year-old, I knew the reason was because my mother has the direct line to God.

Before I went inside our little pop-up, I noticed that our cousin Beth was zooming away in her electric wheelchair to the cinder block bath house to take cover, accompanied by her mother, my Aunt Barb. Barb was not technically my aunt, but in fact my mother's cousin. Due to the age difference I was required by my parents to address all the people who were my second cousins once-removed as "Aunt" and "Uncle."

"Should we go to the bath house?" I asked.

"No," Mom said. "There's glass in there."

I remembered learning about the dangers of glass during tornado weather at school. Four or five times a year, we had tornado drills at Highland Christian, and I loved them. Every so often, the tornado siren rang out for real, and I loved that just as much, if not more. You would think a school of 200 little kids would devolve into a riot of crying and screaming when the lights went out, but our teachers would not allow it. When the siren rang, the kids sitting at the end of the rows next to the windows did exactly what they'd been asked to do: stand up, slide open the small, screened window closest to each of them (this was said to reduce the amount of air pressure building up inside the building, which could cause a building to literally explode) then pull down the enormous black shades over the column of glass blocks that rose to the ceiling above the open windows. Then our teacher would stand by the door as we filed out in an orderly fashion and lined up, facing the wall, in the hallway. Then out came the teacher, who would make sure all of her students were out of the room, and then we all knelt on the floor and covered our heads with our arms, and stayed that way until the principal told us it was safe to get up. Some of the girls said he did this because he liked to roam the hallway and laugh at all of our butts sticking up in the air, but I never believed it. Our principal was stern, but kind and very strong, and liked to help us open our tin cans of chocolate pudding at lunch time, provided we let him keep the metal pull-tab lids so he could lick them clean, because he loved pudding but his wife never let him eat the stuff.

There was no tornado drill for Potato Creek campground. So I sat at the little booth surrounding the pressboard table inside our Starcraft pop-up, where we had eaten breakfast that morning, and took out a book to read. Seconds later, the rain came. If you have never heard rain tapping on the roof of a camper, consider yourself lucky. Even in a light drizzle, it sounds like a million ping pong balls landing on cement. You can hardly hear the other people in the camper speaking to you. Then magically, you step outside, and the rain is as gentle as can be, and you can hear again. This particular rainfall was the worst it had ever been for us, but the most threatening sound was the wind punching the canvas, like a person beating the dust out of a rug. Then the rain on the roof stopped, and switched directions. Dad cracked open the tiny metal door and it almost got away from him.

"It's going sideways now!"

"Bill, SHUT THE DOOR!"

The next thing I knew, the right wing of the pop-up was shaking. I was sitting nearest to it, but my Mom made me switch from the booth to the couch at the other end. Just in time, too, because the wing began to slide inward on its rail, the wind easily knocking out the outside brace like it was nothing more than a toothpick. My dad was there to catch it, and he struggled to push it back into place. He had it half-way back out again, when my mom began shouting at him from the other end of the little room. The left wing had also started sliding in, and was headed right for my head. My mom could not hold it back against the wind by herself. My dad moved to her side and they both tried pushing it back, neither of them strong enough to make much headway. I sat on the couch, because there was nothing I could do, except stay out of the way.

The right wing and left wing were both sliding in, out of control, and pretty soon it was my mom on one side, my dad on the other, both of them just barely able to brace their weight on the platforms hard enough to keep the camper from imploding. It was at least enough to keep the wings on the rails until the rain stopped. I screamed and closed my eyes and put my hands over my ears. It was Mom and Dad vs. nature, and nature was winning. At home, we had a basement. Any time Mom declared the sky looked green, the three of us were down there, huddled in blankets in front of the console television set, watching for signs of funnel clouds on the news radar. Inside the pop-up, the only plan of action was to hold the hell on to your hat. I had to go to into tornado position inside my own head.

The merciful thing about a tornado in your vicinity is the accompanying horrific thunderstorms usually die out quickly. The wind and rain fizzled out as quickly as it had frothed up. I was OK, and so were Mom and Dad. Exhausted, the two of them set to putting things back in place, and bracing the wings as best they could. I stepped outside, and squinted back at the sun that had broken through the clouds. All the campers in our little group were fine. Budweiser party lights had fallen down, a few lawn chairs strewn about, but nobody was harmed. After everyone was accounted for, the adults gathered around the soggy campfire pit to share stories. Everyone was a little shaken up but also a little bit rejuvenated by the near-disaster. Mom joked to Uncle Bill K., still holding his Stroh's inside his favorite koozie.

"Right Bill, it'll blow over, all right. Blow your CAMPER right over." Everybody laughed at that, except Uncle Bill K.

Soon the park rangers in their forest green trucks were making the rounds, asking if we were all OK, and assessing any personal or property damage. Everyone in our area of the grounds was fine, and even a little perplexed at the questions, which the rangers asked with great gravity. Somebody asked what was wrong, and we were told there were lots of overturned campers at the other end of the campground. Gasps from the adults.

After the rangers left, the adults quieted down and waited for one of them to be the first to make the suggestion. It may have been our social director, Aunt Joyce.

In minutes, our group was piled into Uncle Wes's truck, and some others' vans, and we were cruising around to look at the damage. At the east end of the state park, there were indeed several camping vehicles lying on their sides, mostly pop-ups. Lots of upended tents. I am certain our moms and dads and aunts and uncles did more than act like looky-loos; I have no doubt they offered help to the fellow campers who were picking up pieces of damaged property, and more than likely there were offerings of food. But it looked like everyone at this end was simply packing up and going home. We understood that.

As we made our way back to our campsite, however, we noticed it was more than just the worst-hit campers who were packing it in. Everybody was going home. Even the people in giant recreation vehicles who'd been safely sheltered in the trees were getting out of Dodge. In a few hours, the Mesman clan was the only group left at Potato Creek. We were puzzled at this overreaction on the part of the other campers. The rain was over, it was going to be a mild evening, we still had some dry wood, and tomorrow was going to be as fine a day as any to pack up and go home.

Part of me wonders if maybe our insistence on always staying until the bitter end of the weekend had something to do with having an excuse to miss church. But that's probably not it. My dad, and everybody else's dads and some moms had jobs to go back to on Monday. Hard jobs, some dirty jobs, some jobs with true jerks for bosses. Nobody in our clan had a career in which you could point to and say they were living their "passion." Nobody spoke of that back in the 1980s. Jobs were just jobs; their passion was togetherness, and getting away from the suburbs and the traffic, if only for two or three nights.

These were the kinds of vacations our moms and dads could afford; we cousins thought this was completely normal until we expanded our social circle and heard about families who actually went far away and stayed in hotels on vacations, as a rule. Our rule was camping; hotels were an extravagance. I guess even when tornadoes and rain or the humidity of a

Midwest July threatened to spoil everyone's fun, it was better than being at work.

For me, it was the same feeling. Getting sucked up by a twister on a weekend was better than a week spent at school, especially a whole week with no tornado drills. Even if Mom and Dad were not always sure what the best plan of action was, they acted as if they did, for my sake, because that is Love.

Canyon Toe

The great abyss gnawed off and spit back out five of my toes.

Walking appears problematic. Under advisement from my far superior hiking partners – two of whom, Tammy and Julie, are nurses – my feet are relying on the healing powers of a soak in the Colorado River. Never mind that in the process of prying off my boots and peeling away the sweat-saturated double layer of white sport socks from my feet, I stumbled and gashed the inside of my ankle on one of the billion-year-old rocks which we pledged to not disturb during our stay in the Grand Canyon.

"Our stay." I make it sound so crisp and proper, like six adventurous and privileged English spinsters in a Merchant-Ivory film: our wide-brimmed straw hats tied with netting under our chins, protecting our dimpled faces from the desert sun and sand, while our carefully chosen and well-tailored traveling skirts billow out over the broad, strong backs of the canyon mules, which we ride side-saddle of course, with still more mules carrying our matching luggage bringing up the tail end of the party, and we are guided and protected at either end of the single file, downward spiral march by armed members of the Yavapai tribe.

The naive part might be the only description that fits here. At least in my case. Still, the Phantom Ranch, the primitive hikers' campground at the bottom of the Grand Canyon, is a welcome oasis.

I try to enjoy the moment while I can, for tomorrow has its own set of problems. Specifically, as I have stated, the walking thing. But for the moment, I tell myself, I have made it. I hiked to the bottom and I am now soaking in the cold river, and none of the day's regrettable moments matter: the sweating and swearing, hunger and thirst, or pissing while standing up behind a tree because my legs are too weak to squat and the sparse toilets along the trail are out of order because of the water shortage. I made it, and I see the cute Japanese girl we met at the campground yesterday, traveling by herself, has also made it. I had said a little prayer for her when we passed by her on the way down on the South Kaibab earlier today. She was traveling alone and seemed to be muttering to herself about the heat, but had turned down our offer to join our party. Surveying the rest of the campers along our short span of the river, I also thanked God to see that the German couple and the British couple had made it down in one piece.

We'd met and chatted with both couples at one or more rest stops along the eight-mile trek down. All four wore beat-up hiking shoes and eager smiles because they were adventurers on one of their European-style month-long holidays. The two couples talked about all the hiking they'd done in New England and the Pacific Northwest, and how they were not at all intimidated on their first time at the Canyon. But they're European, walking is what they do.

About a mile from the bottom, however, I thought the Germans were going to call it quits. We passed them on one of the many switchbacks on the trail, where they had evidently taken an impromptu rest in a tiny niche in the canyon wall, one of those recesses that offer about six inches of shade from the punishing sun, and yet if you were having a bad moment, you would trade your little sister for a minute of that shade. The tiny German girl was having a moment. As we passed, we could hear great sniffs, the kind you only get with a crying jag. Her boyfriend was kneeling in front of her with a bottle of water, wiping her tears and brushing the wisps of hair off her forehead, saying something undoubtedly sweet to her in German.

I had been in a great deal of pain myself at that point of our trek, and I would have given anything to be in that niche, with my betrothed stroking my face and coaching me into my happy place, attempting to block others from seeing me cry.

At least I maintained a stiff upper lip on the way down here. I may have shrieked, once, at the size of a wasp that hovered near the opening of my water bottle, seasoned with Powerade. Neither did I whine and complain, but I did outright declare that I would for a very long time after this trip avoid consuming any more so-called sports drinks.

Also nice to think about is the fact that I am getting married on October 27. Today it is still the summer of 2001, and I am on vacation in a staggeringly gorgeous place, and a lot of bad things in the world have not yet happened. I had descended into the great abyss with a group of five other women. Jean, an experienced Canyon hiker who was setting out for bible college in the fall at the age of 30; Tammy, an athletic and upbeat neonatal nurse and born-again Christian who shares my weekly addiction to Buffy the Vampire Slayer, though she is more of an Angel girl while I favor Giles; Julie, a sturdy and serious Minnesotan who liked to decorate her house in doilies despite her age being under 60; Pam, the kind and gentle school teacher with a beautiful singing voice; and Jodie, whom I'd never met before but who was an old high school friend of

Jean's. All of them were Calvinettes. Not in the literal sense; I am fairly certain their non-denominational preachers – who favored pacing around with headsets in front of congregations gathered in rooms that resembled warehouses more than they resembled church sanctuaries – would never approve of the concept of predestination. But definitely these girls were Calvinettes in the symbolic and behavioral sense.

All were good, clean Americans who never swore and had adequately trained themselves for the journey into one of the great wonders of the earth. And then there was the 28-year-old out-of-shape slacker who just came along to see the Grand Canyon for the first time. That would be me.

We had embarked on an early morning trek down the South Kaibab Trail from the south, a trail known for its breathtaking views that far exceed those of the Bright Angel Trail, a much wider, safer and widely used trail that hugs the side of the canyon. The Kaibab, on the other hand, juts out into the canyon. It is much more narrow, less populated with tourists, and steep.

We had already stayed one night on the piney, secluded North Rim, where we had left our rental mini-van and traveled via the Trans-Canyon Shuttle around to the South Rim. The plan was to hike the South Kaibab down, stay a night at the Phantom Ranch, continue north on the Kaibab and stay a second night in the canyon at some waterfall before hiking out to the North Rim.

I had practiced hiking uphill with a heavy backpack, and even broken in my expensive new hiking boots, boots I resented having to purchase in the first place but did so after months of haranguing by the rest of my party, even though I was convinced I could do the whole canyon thing in my Birkenstocks. I packed lightly and efficiently. I trimmed my toenails extra short. I did everything I thought I was supposed to do to prepare for this trip. What I did not possess was a pair of the special moisture-wicking socks, apparently sold at the same establishment at which I'd bought my boots.

And so, the most auspicious companion of mine on this trip are the Wrong Socks.

I had assumed that hiking down hill all day would be a breeze, and that hiking back out the next day would be the hard part. But an entire day descending into a hotter and hotter canyon has shown me just how far in over my head I am. Wearing two pairs of simple white sport socks, my toes had begun throbbing half-way through the eight-hour descent. Or maybe it was 10 hours. Either way, I am in trouble.

Sitting alone on the bank of the river to inspect my wounds, I see the strange and unnatural happening in the toe region. My heart is in my throat and I try not to panic. At least five of my toenails, including the ones on each of my big toes, are solid white. I touch them with the tip of my finger and it is like nudging a loose tooth. One false move and those nails will be off and sailing down the river.

Then comes the fear. Then the dread. There is no way to hide this from the nurses. I am going to have to be straight with them, because I am clearly injured and we are going to have to make a decision as a group. Then comes the guilt.

Tammy and Pam and Julie assure me I should not panic, and that I should keep soaking my feet in the water. One of them later helps me bandage up my toes for the night. But Jean – not a nurse – takes the tough love approach with me. She begins the third degree: questioning me about my socks, about the length of my toenails, about whether my boots had been adequately broken in.

"Didn't you buy the moisture-wicking socks?" she asks.

"Moisture ... what-ing?" is my reply.

This diminutive woman who bravely bears a Jesus fish on the bumper of her Geo in her home city, a city in which the majority of people are secular humanists, some of whom have flipped her off for wearing her religion on her car, a fact that compels her to live her life in constant vigilance of the example she is setting for Jesus and therefore NEVER uses swear words, quite off-handedly says to the group that night, "I don't know how the hell we're going to get out of here."

In more ways than I can count, I have truly hit bottom. I have made Jean swear.

The next morning, the six of us load up our gear and make our way along the path that would lead us to the Kaibab Trail headed north. Our plan has been to hike out to the North Rim, where we had left our rental van, and head back home after a night in Las Vegas.

About one-tenth of a mile along, I know I am not going to make it. It is early morning, the air is cool and dry, but I am sweating profusely and my feet are completely numb. The ranger's cabin is within sight. Jean and Pam accompany me to front door, where I knock, only to receive no answer. I remind myself that it is early, and we wait. After about 10 agonizing minutes, agonizing mostly in the sense that it gives me time to think about my embarrassing situation and to wonder about how many times these rangers get woken up by some hapless injured tourist, I am greeted by a tall, red-haired woman named Pam Cox. As she asks me questions, she wraps up my toes and gives me some extra bandages.

During this time I stare at her badge and swear to never forget her name. She tells me the moisture inside my boots, combined with the constant downhill motion, has pummeled and pickled my toes, and that I will, over the next two weeks, probably lose all of my toenails. "But they'll grow back," she says. Then she asks me if I have any other shoes I can wear besides hiking boots, and I say yes, I have also brought a pair of Birkenstocks. Good, she says, you'll wear those instead.

"So ..." I say, "You're not going to evacuate me?" Mind you, the helicopter that evacuates the sick, injured or dead costs said sick and injured or dead individuals upwards of $1,000 per trip.

The ranger says to me, "We don't evacuate Canyon Toe. You got yourself down here, you can get yourself out. Just take the Bright Angel back up to the South Rim, and take someone with you."

"Canyon Toe?"

"It's fairly common," she says, and I can almost see the thought bubble above her head adding, "among chubby vacationers who don't know the difference between hiking the canyon and deciding to take the stairs at the shopping mall."

There is something weirdly reassuring about having a name for my injuries, and knowing that other dumb hikers had gotten themselves out of the canyon.

So. That leaves the six of us with a decision to make. Jean makes the decision for all of us, this time without the swearing. She volunteers to stay behind with me at Phantom Ranch. The rangers give us a pass for an extra night, due to my circumstances, and Jean agrees see me out of the canyon safely the following day.

With hugs and much encouragement, especially from Tammy ("Remember you're a vampire slayer! You can do anything!"), we say goodbye to the rest of our party, and rest up for the remainder of the day.

The next morning at 2 a.m., it is time to go. My pack is scheduled to go up by mule, and Jean decides to be my virtual mule by carrying all the food and water in her pack to keep the extra weight off my feet. Though most hikers schedule two days to climb up and out of the canyon, we have to do it in one day if we are meant to rest up on the South Rim for a night before catching the shuttle back to the North Rim to meet up with our party.

The climb out takes us 17 hours.

Seventeen hours of throbbing feet, trembling leg muscles, maddening switchbacks and plenty of odd looks from other athletic and keen hikers with their backs piled high with high tech camping gear. Here I am, the taller and bigger of the pair of us, and Jean, all of 5'2", is the only one of us carrying a pack. And there I am, in white socks covered in red dust and black Birkenstock sandals.

Jean is patient with me, because what else could one be in this situation? But she does not baby me. Mostly we try making conversation during the more boring parts of the hike. During the hard parts, when I have to stop every five minutes to rest my shaking muscles, she is calm, but prodding. She only lets me rest for two minutes at a time when we are between rest areas, and at times I hate her for it. Other times I gush, thanking her for making this sacrifice, and other times, I apologize for throwing a wrench into her plans. Plenty of people in her situation would lie to me and say, "Oh, it's OK. Don't worry about it. I'm just glad I was here to help." Jean makes it clear to me that there was no other choice, and she makes no bullshit about the seriousness of the situation that I'd gotten myself into.

The unspoken truth between us is that weeks before the trip, Jean had confronted me about her doubts in my ability to make this hike. I had assured her I was training for it. I knew I had slacked in my training, but I just wanted Jean to stop bugging me about it. What I really wanted was to see the Grand Canyon, and I had foolishly placed my trust in my endurance and my ability to tolerate a little pain. Bless Jean, she never reminds me of that conversation we had had weeks earlier. She does not need to. It plays on a loop in my mind for 17 hours while she practically cattle-prods me out of that canyon.

When we are about a half mile from the trail head, I am utterly exhausted. My legs are shutting down. I have never felt quite so tired before. I cannot move a muscle, and I cannot tolerate yet another switchback – those parts of the trail that give the illusion that you are not getting anywhere, because the trail switches directions back and forth along the broad side of a steep hill. The switchbacks are potentially crazy-making, because you can see the top of the hill just a few feet above your head, and you want to break from the trail and climb straight up, but you do not do it because you know it is too steep, and karma is not in your favor.

As I rest my tush on the last of many, many 4 billion-year-old red rocks, the pair of English hikers approach us. They, too, are on their way out after a night at Phantom Ranch with us, and after camping their second night half-way up the Bright Angel Trail at Indian Gardens, where Jean and I had only stopped for lunch earlier today. My mental anguish is obvious, as I am close to tears. The English guy and his girlfriend talk to Jean for a minute. I do not register what they are saying to each other. All I can think about is how all the walking in baggy shorts has chafed my inner thighs so badly they feel like raw chicken, and therefore must also look like it, and I wonder if I should pray for a miracle from the Lord to pick me up, dust me off, shower me and deposit me in a hospital bed because I surely cannot get there under my own strength.

Then the English guy, a tall person with the inexplicable pretty face that somehow only foreign guys possess (probably because I project this onto them; I always did have crushes on the exchange students when I was in school), speaks to me with that accent that would on any other day knock my incompetent white sport socks off.

It is not a miracle from heaven, but instead it is a lovely hallucination. I am having a vision of Rupert Giles from Buffy the Vampire Slayer. Rupert Giles, the Watcher, upon seeing the dire circumstances of his vampire-slaying charge, closes the spell book he is reading to regard my situation, calm and stoic and Englishy. He kneels down in front of me in his three-piece tweed suit so I can see his face. The tweed is getting all red and dusty from kneeling on the ground, but he ignores that. He sets down his ceramic “Kiss the Librarian” mug of PG Tips hot tea on a nearby rock, then removes his wire-rimmed glasses for dramatic effect, looks me in the eye, and says, "Buffy, look how far you have come, in bloody Birkenstock sandals no less. This is nothing. You blew up the evil mayor/giant snake thing on graduation day. You tore the power source out of Adam's steel-plated chest with your bare hand. And The Master bloody well drowned you and you came back to life!"

"Yeah, I guess," I croak. Then I snap out of it and see that an actual British guy not in tweed, but in cargo shorts, is talking to me.

"You’re literally steps away from the top and you’re going to make it. You’re a rock star!” he says.

I nod my head pitifully and thank him as he and his girlfriend move on ahead of us. Jean and I indeed make it out in just a few minutes after that.

She and I lose touch over the years. I get married and move to Texas. Jean goes on to Bible college and mission work somewhere in Papua New Guinea. I credit her for saving my life, even though, as she pointed out, there was no other choice. I am sure that any one of the women in our party could have seen me out of the canyon just fine, but Jean's approach to me was starkly different from what Tammy's would have been. Tammy and I could have spent 17 hours talking about television shows, and I would have loved her for it. Jean was not exactly mean to me, but neither did she hold my hand. She does not need to watch television, because she herself is a superhero.

As a person who has floated from one unsatisfying and underpaid journalism job to another just to pay bills, it is a constant battle with myself to sit down and write what I love. I love to write fiction, but I am in the middle of the desert on at least three different projects. Each of them has initially inspired me to run with it for as long as I can. Then I get to the bottom, where the real work begins. If I look up and try to figure out how far I have to go, I lose hope. The desert can really sap a girl of her energy.

Hiking out of the Grand Canyon is the hardest thing I have ever done. However, I have to remind myself that I did do it. I finished it. If you will graciously allow me to stretch that metaphor just a little bit further: I am sure now that if I can drag my tired butt out of one of the natural wonders of the world, then I can bloody well finish writing a book, and write it well.

Grease, Pain and Chicago 17

I step up the bus stairs, and the smell of exhaust gives way to the morning breath, perfume and hairspray of 40 Highland Christian School kids, some watching me make my way to the near-back. Not to the very back with the bad-ass eighth grade posse. And not quite to the second or third row from the back, with our fellow seventh grade classmates, Jeff, Pete and Mike. Instead, Tracy, my pre-arranged friend since the fourth grade, is sitting there in the "Near North" neighborhood of the back of the bus.

Because of me, Tracy's not quite cool enough to sit with the cool crowd. It just figures that the power triumvirate of my class would have to ride the same bus as I do. With my pink Chuck Taylor high tops, pathetic rat-tail hairdo and Duran Duran stickers all over my Trapper Keeper, I bring down Tracy's ability to be a fully-realized "*Heather*."

Tracy's definitely got a Shannen Doherty quality. The prom queen potential is there. Tracy's mother works for a cosmetics company, so Tracy has always had a drawerful of new lipsticks, even as a sixth-grader. She seems to know a lot more about skin care than I do, and never hesitates to inform me of how unusual it is that she has brown eyes, olive skin and blonde hair, making her a "summer," and of how I am pale, round of face and blue of eye, ergo a "spring," which is very, very average. I also know, because Tracy has told me, that her slender, tan wrists are the perfect complement to gold tennis bracelets. This is why she will not waste her time with the colored plastic jelly bracelets that I buy with the intention of trading and sharing with her. I am not sure why anyone would care about wearing jewelry while playing sports, especially tennis. If anything, it seems to me it would make things more dangerous. My softball coach, whom we called Miss Van, always makes us take off our jewelry when we play.

When we were younger, and Tracy's family moved to our neighborhood, our moms were over the moon about the idea that two Highland Christian classmates would live so close together. At the time I thought this was a dumb reason to be friends with anybody. In fact, I know my mom has been out of her mind for years already because she is always pressuring me to be friends with this boy Eric, who ranks about as high as I do on the cool spectrum. I rarely speak to boys, except to yell at them to leave me alone, and to inform them of their inferior intellect. And besides, Eric is always sitting behind me in social studies, whispering snide comments to me.

"Why did you get that stupid rat tail in your hair? It looks stupid." No amount of telling him to shut up worked. "I'm going to cut that thing off," he'd say.

But even I had to admit the friendship with Tracy was perfect timing back in the fourth grade. Christina, my other neighborhood friend, was a year older than I and was getting a little tired of me asking if I could come over to listen to her older sister's "Grease" movie soundtrack on their parents' living room stereo.

This record, by the way, was the same record I had begged and begged my parents to buy for me, but they had been hesitant, as they were nervous about me listening to the "rock music." Then one Christmas morning, my well-meaning mom watched me as I opened a record that did in fact have the word "Grease" on the cover, but the picture was a cartoonish group of little kids dressed vaguely like they were on their way to a 1950s costume day at school during Spirit Week. My heart dropped a little as I saw no sign of my beloved Danny Zuko or Knicky anywhere.

"Thanks, Mom," I said, knowing the consequences of telling her the truth about something she had bought for me. When I put that thing on the record player, it was nothing even close to the "Grease" soundtrack. What I wanted was the show tunes from the tawdry but lovable Broadway musical made into a film starring Vinny Barbarino.

This record was a litany of simpering, third-rate covers of 1950s songs about cars and puppy love and other dumb shit. Now that I look back on it, I wonder if my mom was just trying to avoid being the mother who allowed her daughter to listen to songs in which innocent girls are accused of getting "friendly down in the sand," and who were criticized for being "lousy with virginity."

Either way, Christina and her sisters were too mature for me, and I could see it in their eyes whenever I came over, though they were too nice to outright ditch me.

Tracy and I, on the other hand, were in the same class, and she had no older sisters to corrupt me. So naturally we ought to be best friends. And we were, for a time. We used to ride bikes together all over Griffith and the safer parts of Gary in the summers, go exploring in the wild patches around our sad little neighborhood playground, practice flips on the steel jungle gyms that left our palms smelling like rust.

In bad weather, Tracy and I would spend our hours together indoors, playing with my single-speaker radio/tape player, the precursor to the mighty boombox. When I figured out I could press down the plastic buttons marked "play" and "record" at the same time, and actually make recordings of myself talking, and of the TV, I thought I had discovered the secret to true happiness.

We would record each other telling stories, giving news reports, or replaying scenes from Growing Pains and Degrassi Junior High.

We tried getting Christina in on this action with a little Star Wars re-enactment, but she got bored with it pretty quickly. Mostly, it was just Tracy and me, playing back our recordings and cackling hysterically at how stupid we sounded. These sessions were frequently interrupted by Tracy having to hobble to the bathroom, shouting, "stop making me laugh!"

Lately, though, Tracy and I have been getting bored of recording ourselves, and more interested in listening to the radio and watching MTV. She will watch Duran Duran videos with me, but I am not allowed to tell anybody else that she does this. Everybody else in our class thinks Duran Duran is gay, because of the makeup and the good clothes. But Tracy is unashamed about her love of the band Chicago. Specifically, the Chicago 17 album. Somehow she has gotten her hands on the cassette. I in my blossoming pre-amateur-deejay years have also obtained the same album, but by very different means. I have recorded each and every song off the radio. It is a lot easier to do than it sounds. Every radio station in 1986 is playing "You're the Inspiration" every five minutes. I am also not above holding my cassette recorder's microphone up to the speakers on the television while I watch MTV until my arms ache, an activity that Tracy finds weird and babyish.

Today I find Tracy in the usual bus seat, with the usual empty space next to her on the greenish pleather cushions that look and smell like giant rubber erasers. As the bus starts to move again, I use my school bag to keep my balance as I plod down the aisle toward my friend. I get ready to plop myself in next to her, but I am stopped short by her tan, polished hand on the seat.

"You can't sit here," Tracy's two eyebrows come together as one.

Oh, it's one of those days, I think.

"Why not?"

There is no sign of a forthcoming "just kidding!" accompanied by a crazy Muppet smile to throw her tiny beauty freckle out of whack. She is totally serious. I shrug and sit in the seat across the aisle from her, and ask her what is wrong.

"If you don't know, I'm not going to tell you."

When I get older, I will observe irrational people saying this exact phrase to their spouses when they themselves do not know why they are angry. Tracy uses it on me at least once a month. I do not particularly like her all the time, either, but there is usually an obvious reason.

"Are you mad at me?"

"Took you long enough to figure that out," she says.

"Tracy, what is wrong?"

"Don't talk to me."

And so it goes.

Tracy has been having a lot of days like this lately. She acts mad, will not say why, but puts it on me to figure it out. Sometimes she lashes out because I failed to call her on the phone to talk the night before. Sometimes there is no explanation. But always, it ends the same. She will phone me after school, or approach me at recess while I am alone, tossing a softball against the red brick wall of the junior high wing, and simply say, "Sorry."

I always say, "It's OK." But it is not OK. I want to know what her problem is, but she never, not even once, will explain her behavior, or explain what I might have done. This will go on and on until ninth grade, when we have both gone on to the same high school and the same bus route, again. She will pull the same shit, again, on the bus, again. But by that time, I will have had enough, and we will never speak again. Then she will be free to make her move on a slightly larger, less familiar popular crowd, who have not yet connected her to me.

Until high school, she and I are stuck with the same 27 faces we have known since Kindergarten.

Tracy is mad all the way through morning recess today. Then before lunch, our Bible teacher gives our classmate Rachel permission to make an announcement that will change everything. For me, for Tracy, and for everybody else in the class.

Rachel, who is famous for her awesome, awake-all-night slumber parties, has apparently moved on from celebrating with just us girls, who dance around to Prince and Olivia Newton-John with our nightshirts tied on like halter tops until we are exhausted and it is time for Light as a Feather, Stiff as a Board. Today, Rachel indeed announces she is having a party. But this time, everyone is invited. Boys too. But not for sleeping over.

"Just for pizza, ice cream and music and stuff."

Music and stuff? I know instantly what that is going to be. There will be dancing. More importantly, there will be socializing with Pete, Jeff and Mike. These are not people I would normally care to hang out with, but then I never had the opportunity before. I am going to that party, even if that means I must go by myself. I know those boys are out of my league, friendship-wise, and I also know that they intimidate the crap out of me. Jeff's not so bad to people, just silent most of the time, but then laughs easily when others are subject to his friends' ridicule. Pete can be ruthless in making fun of my Duran Duran stickers. Mike is ... more complicated. Mike has no pimples and giant white teeth that he rarely shows because he seems to enjoy looking tough. Usually he just looks like he is thinking about basketball, or considering whether he might be outgrowing his Guess sweatshirt. So help me, I cannot deny it. I have a crush on the most popular boy in our class, for absolutely no good reason. He will be the first of many, many unfitting crushes.

Tracy comes up to me during recess while I am hanging upside down on the monkey bars to make the blood rush to my head, one of the other things she is no longer interested in doing with me.

"Sorry."

"It's OK."

"Are we going to Rachel's party?" she asks.

I swing off the bar and stand upright, holding on to the bar just in case I black out. This is definitely a grown up conversation, and one should probably not be upside down while having it.

"I don't care," I say with a shrug, kicking the dirt around on the ground with the rubber toes of my Chuck Taylors. "Why, you wanna go?"

Tracy folds her arms in front of her. "I don't want to go to that. I'm not going to any party with those snobs. Michelle and Liz aren't even going."

"Really? Why not?" Our classmates Michelle and Liz are two other girls who also teeter on the fringe: Michelle teeters because she is so studious she does not have much time for a social life, but she is saved from ridicule because of her kindness, good looks, charm and athleticism. Liz totters much further on the end of the cool scale. She is our class's lone Presbyterian who sketches for fun and takes opera lessons. Tracy puts up with Michelle because there is no real reason not to like her. She puts up with Liz because Michelle is Liz's friend and protector.

"I guess you're right," I say. "My parents probably won't let me, anyway."

"Why do you gotta do everything your parents say?"

"I don't do everything my parents say."

"Yes you do."

"Shut up!"

"Don't tell me to shut up! You shut up."

And there the tiff picks up where it has left off.

Tracy phones that evening to say she is sorry. And then I tell her that we are going to the party.

Between this day and the day of the party, I get a dozen phone calls from Tracy every night, regarding what we might be wearing. My mother likes to dress me like a nun for special events, so Tracy wants to make sure I'm not going to embarrass her. We settle on the lightest pair of dark blue K-Mart jeans that I own. I pair this with a boring sweater, as every other top I own has a dippy white collar that my mom calls Peter Pan or something. Of course, nobody wants to look at the only really cool thing I have to wear, the thing that I would wear to a party if even one person there thought I was cool enough: a white linen blazer in the yachting fashion of the "Her Name is Rio" video. I dare not. Many years later, I will wish that I had dared.

Mom helps me with my hair and makeup on the night of the party, because I am so nervous I might throw up. There is not much to be done with my short hair other than a classic feathering. When she finishes, I peer into the mirror and decide

I look like somebody's pudgy little sister, and not anything close to resembling Mallory Keaton, which is the preppy look I was going for.

The good news is I have my Kodak Disk camera, which is the latest thing, I think. Everybody at the party will think it is cool, and now I have a chance to practice with it.

The practicing with my camera at the party does not go well. Very little is going on other than people pairing up and slow dancing, with Tracy and I watching from the sofa in the corner by the stereo. It is dark, and I am determined to use this new camera, so the flash is a little bit off-putting to the other people. Because I have no other nerd friends at the party besides Tracy, it has been determined that I have a crush on somebody. And because I am the spaz that I am, nobody believes for a second that I brought my camera to record this historic event for the fun of it. It is further determined by the hive mind of the cool kids at the party that my affection is directed at one person in particular.

"Watch out, Mike, somebody has a crush on you," says Pete, and all the dancing couples turn to me and laugh or smirk in puzzlement. Mike pretends to freak out and dashes under the snack table, acting as if hiding from a stalker. I put the camera away, and am now agitated and have no occupation. Nobody is dancing with me, nobody is coming anywhere near me or Tracy.

The beginning chords of "You're the Inspiration" come on the stereo, and Tracy shoots me a glare that makes me wish I was somewhere else entirely. She seems to be reading my thoughts precisely because she says, "Why did we come here?"

"I thought you wanted to come to the party."

"No, I didn't. I decided to come because you wanted to come."

"Why would I want to come here? None of these people like me even a little bit."

"I've been asking myself the same thing."

"But you never said anything. If you knew it was going to go like this, why didn't you stop me?"

"Because we always do what you want to do. You always get your way and now we're stuck at this dumb party with no boys who like us, and my favorite song is on the radio and I'm so depressed I want to gag myself with your stupid camera."

"Well, excu-uuse me." I have developed neither wit nor backbone at the age of 13. Other than what I have gleaned from Saturday Night Live re-runs.

I am quiet for a minute and I listen to the song. Despite my humiliation, the song still reminds me of the beach. Every song on the Chicago 17 album reminds me of laying on a blanket at the Indiana Dunes in the summer. Soon it will be summer again, and maybe my dad or an aunt will take me there again. I will lie down on my back and close my eyes, listening to the waves, and to some older girls nearby, flirting with the lifeguards, and to eleven different boomboxes, all at once, and eventually I will hear Chicago. I will keep listening with my eyes closed, pretending that my skin is not ghost pale, and that I am not wearing a chubby girl swimsuit with the little frill on the bottom that accentuates the width of my hips. I will also pretend that the suntan lotion I am wearing was not slathered on my back by an older relative, but by a boy, and not any boy whom I have known since Kindergarten, and he will not be known by anybody in my stupid class at school or at church or at Calvinettes. This boy is so new he cares about none of those ordinary things, and he likes the fact that my mom cuts my hair and that I have Duran Duran posters on my wall. He also thinks jelly bracelets are cool, and he wears tons of black ones on each wrist, and we give each other a new jelly bracelet for every day we have been going out. I also pretend that I live not on Indiana Street in a ranch house, but in a huge, old, three-story plantation house surrounded by ancient trees. Somewhere in Florida. And this boy will climb our trees at midnight on my birthday, all the way up to the highest dormer window, and peek into my attic bedroom, where I will be pretending to be asleep, and he will know that I am pretending but he will let me pretend, and I will know that he knows I am pretending, but I will keep pretending until the song ends.

"Are you listening to me?"

"No." I have yet to develop the ability to lie out of politeness.

It is then that I notice that the rest of the party-goers have ambled upstairs to the kitchen for ice cream, and Tracy and I seem to be alone.

"Figures."

"Do you want me to call my dad to pick us up?"

"No way," Tracy says. "We'd look even dorkier if we leave now."

"Why?"

"I'm going upstairs for some ice cream with everyone else. Are you coming?"

"No."

"Fine crybaby."

The fact is, I am not crying. But somehow the mention of crying, combined with my best friend abandoning me for ice cream, does make me cry.

And then, the song changes to "Hard For Me To Say I'm Sorry." I keep this opinion from Tracy, but I believe this one is a much better Chicago song than "You're the Inspiration." For one thing, there are a lot more things going on with the melody, whereas "Inspiration" sort of plods along predictably, like your average 1980s love song. Also, the words are a lot more interesting. "Inspiration" is a straight forward, candy-coated declaration of love. It would be embarrassing, frankly, to listen to some guy sing that to me out loud in public. "Hard For Me To Say I'm Sorry," however, is a song about a guy who screwed up, and is apparently very stubborn about the fact that he screwed up, but he loves the girl anyway, so he is just going to leave it up to her to decide no matter how much it hurts. If somebody wrote that for me, I'd instantly throw my life away and ride off into the sunset on his motorcycle.

"Inspiration" is a simple sugar. "Hard For Me To Say I'm Sorry," is a complex carbohydrate, and therefore much more satisfying.

Great song or not, I will not be dancing anytime soon.

"You wanna dance?"

The voice is impatient, with a hint of annoyance. The question is put to me as if somebody's mother has forced him to be nice to me.

I look up. It is Eric, my mother's favorite person. He is the skinny boy who sits behind me at school, throwing tiny bits of wadded up notebook paper in my hair, yet still my parents see fit to include his family in our massive campouts. Maybe my mom feels sorry for him because his parents are weird and they never let him or his sister eat candy or do anything fun after 6 o'clock.

I wipe the tears off my cheeks, even though I am past caring if Eric sees me crying or not because I really do not like him.

"You only want to dance with me because you feel sorry for me."

"Yeah, so?"

"Fine."

And we dance.

"Dance" is an incredibly loose term for what we are doing. This is slower than slow dancing, because neither of us know exactly what we are supposed to do. My two hands are on his shoulders, and his two hands are balled up like fists, resting in the general area of my waist. Our bodies remain about two feet apart, and we are sort of rocking back and forth in a vague fashion. We have enough room between us for us both to have been wearing Kool-Aid Man costumes, and indeed it would have made our dancing no less sexy or graceful.

I suddenly have no idea what the puritanical minds of some church people have against dancing. This is about as sensuous an act as putting away the groceries. Because really, what is this, other than Eric doing his duty as a nice person? The thing is, I do not know if he qualifies as one of the nice people. Or at least, I have never thought of him as a nice person.

In the weeks following the party, I think less and less about the buffoons and more about whether Eric is a nice guy. My mom is always telling me that a boy who puts paper in my hair is a boy who likes me. He does make fun of me and pull my rat-tail sometimes. Like the others in school, he does make fun of my Duran Duran obsession, but he does so quietly, not for the benefit of other people.

And, one thing I do like about him is he, like me, is a slacker with the religious doctrine. He never memorizes his Heidelberg Catechism or Bible verses, relieving me from being the sole focus of our assigned church elder's weekly Sunday diatribes. I like that in a boy.

As the school year ends, Eric's annoying behavior continues. But I do stop reacting to him.

"When are you gonna cut off that stupid tail?" he whispers in class one day, flicking my rat-tail with the eraser end of his pencil. Instead of turning around and freaking out on him, I just sit there, pretending to be in rapt attention toward Mr. Deters.

I am blushing.

Eric continues, "I'm gonna cut that thing off with my pocket knife."

I turn and smirk at him. When I turn back around to face the front, Tracy is across the aisle, watching me. She is seeing that my cheeks are pink, and an evil smile spreads across her face. She knows. I get even redder.

"Shut up," I mouth to her, but she is already covering up her mouth and shaking, like she has just heard the most hilarious story and can hardly keep herself from busting up out loud in class. I give her the "don't you dare" look, but she is way past the point of seriousness.

At recess, I corner her. "What were you laughing about?"

"YOU LIKE ERIC!" She is yelling and I am terrified.

"No, I don't."

"YES YOU DO! HE DANCED WITH YOU AT THE PARTY AND NOW YOU'VE DECIDED YOU LIKE HIM."

"No, I haven't and SHUT UP!"

Tracy spends many days at school tormenting me. Literally, she points and laughs silently whenever she sees me anywhere within 10 feet of Eric. When she does this, I think about the fact that I have another entire year to be friends with this person, and I doubt I can stand it.

What I do not know right now is that by next fall, I will be spending a lot more time with other girls in school, especially

Michelle and Liz. I also do not know that I will become even more of an outcast in high school, but I will still have Liz and, eventually, a large group of hilarious, eccentric, brilliant nerd friends. I also cannot foresee that I will stop caring what people think of my hair, my clothes, and what music I listen to, and I have yet to learn that I will eventually, one day, stop putting up with bad friends.

But seventh grade is a pain you have to endure. If I could see into the future, I would also see Tracy hopping from one random boyfriend to another, rarely seeming to get too close to any other girls in high school, and even more rarely cracking a smile on her perfect heart-shaped face. If I could see these things, I might feel sorry for her. I might go a little easier on her when she does what she does. But our inability to prognosticate is a gift. Without a crystal ball, it is easier for me to pull away from Tracy when she does the unthinkable. She tells Eric that I like him.

There is nothing in it for her except a sadistic enjoyment in seeing me freak out, or worse, seeing me in pain. It would be one thing if she was just one of the other people at the party. She has been my best friend for the past four years. And now the entire class knows that my affections have shifted from one boy to another, even though hardly a single one of them who is enjoying this fact has ever bothered to get to know me as a person.

I stay away from Tracy until the end of school, and start spending more time with Liz. Liz, who sings arias whenever she feels like it and references films I have never seen starring Cary Grant, teaches me how to stop caring that people know one single dumb fact about me. On the last day of school, we are all passing around our Highland Christian School yearbooks for signatures. At the end of the day, as we all gather for an assembly in the gym, and I feel relieved knowing I will be at home with my MTV and my Tiger Beat magazines in just another hour, and that I will only have to look at these people once a week for the entire summer, at church. Unless I fake an illness. Mom always falls for that.

Eric hands me my yearbook and sits down on a bleacher in front of me. I open it to the page where he has signed his name. There, he writes: "I think you are a nice girl even though you like me."

I had been beyond caring what Tracy or Eric thought. Or I thought so, until I see now that Eric does not hate my guts even though Tracy told him the truth. In fact, he is not entirely repulsed by me. It is not an affirmation, and it is certainly not the same boy in my dreams who climbs my imaginary tree and gives me jelly bracelets. But it is something. He has made an effort to ease my embarrassment, in his own 13-year-old boy way. And that is better than saying anything out loud about it.

Letters From Home

WARNING, THIS IS THE MOST PITIFULLY WRITTEN AND TYPED LETTER TO EVER MAKE USE OF THE U.S. POSTAL SERVICE.

This was typed in all capital letters on the first of a four-sheaf tome, positioned as the first thing the recipient sees when removing the pages from the envelope. The letter is postmarked 21 August, 1991, and is the very first correspondence I received from home during my freshman year at Dordt College in Sioux Center, Iowa. It came from my cousin, Stephanie, who is in fact my double cousin.

If you have never encountered such a relationship before, let me just start by pointing out that there is nothing backwoods or illegal about such a thing. It just means that her mom and my dad are brother and sister, and her dad and my mom are brother and sister. My usual explanation of this is as follows: Bill married Harriet (Herbie) who is the sister of Wes, who married Bev, who is the sister of Bill.

OK, well, maybe that makes it sound even worse than the hand gestures I use to explain the situation to the People Of The Small Families: the urge is irresistible for me to hold both my hands in the air, making a sort-of peace sign with both hands. My left hand represents one family, the right hand represents the other, *unrelated*, family. My left index finger is my dad, my left middle finger is my aunt; my right index finger is my mom, and right middle finger is my uncle. Then I cheerfully and innocently declare, "See? Brother and sister married brother and sister!" Then I make the corresponding fingers kiss each other.

I do not know if the silent, polite grinning I receive when people see my fingers kissing each other is the result of their brains trying to untie the knots in our family tree, or if they are simply trying to placate a crazy, and potentially chromosomally challenged, individual.

All you need to know is, nobody in my family ever married anybody they were related to. At least as far as we know.

If you are from a big clan, or come from one of those ever-rarer ethnic American enclaves whose members tend to be born, grow up, get married and raise their own kids within the same 20-square-mile area, then you are rolling your eyes right now. "Of course there's nothing weird about double cousins! Why are you wasting your time explaining all of this?"

My response is two-fold: Because I have a tendency to give way more information than necessary to whoever will listen (as demonstrated in the aforementioned visual aid); and because there is something very, VERY weird about me and my own double cousin.

Before I go on, I should point out that Stephanie is not my only double cousin. She has one younger sister, Kim, and a younger brother, Todd. Stephanie and I are three years apart, which meant that we fought like hyenas until I was about 15. It also means that Kim and Todd are quite a bit younger than I am, so although I love them all equally, and we get along and have had great times together, I am not quite cool enough to be their BFFs. Or it could be that Stephanie and I are just too weird together.

As demonstrated by this letter, which found me utterly homesick among the corn fields of Northwest Iowa in the height of my flannelled grunge rock years. Along the bottom of the cover page, Stephanie typed:

He's a little nowhere man, sitting in his nowhere land, making all his nowhere plans for nobody

She goes on to quote from "The Long and Winding Road," "Octopus's Garden," (The Beatles are her favorite band of all time) and "Sleepy Jean," a nod to my inexplicable Monkees infatuation, despite my otherwise impeccable taste in music, and she concludes this first page with

And that's all the songs I can remember. (I hate this stupid typewriter.)

The letter starts off:

Hi Jen (or is it Jenn?)!

I reinvented myself when I went to college as "Jenn" instead of "Jen." The second "n" was very important to me. Just like Ann Shirley in "Ann of Green Gables" always tried to convince people she needed an "e" at the end of Ann to romance it up a bit. Although, honestly, if anybody is the Ann Shirley in this scenario, it would be Stephanie, she of the gorgeous red hair, and I would be her bosom friend Diana.

Well how are things in sodium heaven? excuse me I mean Dordt.

Before you begin to think that somehow in addition to corn and soybeans, that Northwest Iowan farmers also provide us with salt, let me just say, don't be stupid. And then let me say to the rest of you who guessed this is an inside joke, congratulations. The elemental abbreviation for sodium is "Na." That, as everyone knows, is code for Nice Ass.

I had my first class with Frau (or however you spell it) today. She told me that Kristen and Shelley called yesterday. She said that from the way they talked that 90 percent of Dordt's students are of the male gender. Lucky Duck. I am seriously considering a career in Agriculture.

This would be a joke of course. Fifteen years later, Stephanie would begin dating a man who owned his own house that apparently needed some yard work done. When he jokingly asked her to bring over her gardening gloves for a day of fun, she wrote to me, "I'm not doing yard work. Not for any man." She goes on in the letter to talk about her German and journalism classes, both with the Frau.

I think I might like journalism. I'd better, I had it engraved on my ring. She also said something about your mother's teary farewell. How Harlequin Romance-ish.

That report from Frau, always a stickler for accuracy, was correct. I do believe my mother's actual words were, "M-m-my baby d-d-doesn't n-n-need me anym-m-more!" I could not get her out of the dorm fast enough. On the other hand, the bulletin from Frau's twin daughters that there seemed to be nine boys for every girl at our little Christian college was not so much by-the-book, journalistically speaking. Once you remove the undateables from the equation (i.e., the students who show up to college already engaged, the doughy farm boys who are more skilled at removing hog testes than sweeping girls off their feet (and why would you not eliminate a hog testicle removing champion from the dating pool?). It was more like three girls to every guy. And not just any girls. The place was lousy with Calvinettes. Nice, sweet girls who were about 80 percent more dateable than I was.

The thing I wonder about is how Grandpa, being the speedy little worker he is, made your loft. We have a betting pool back here. I put money on two-and-a-half days. Well anyway, it is so #@!$%&**?! hot here right now that you may instantaneously combust on the sidewalk. It's gotta be at least 100 degrees outside. It's terrible and since we go to such a thrifty school I may melt sitting in Mr. O's homeroom. And speeking of your alma-mater (or however you spell it)

Interesting that she seems so concerned about misspelling the Latin phrase for mother school, but not so worried about the fact that I am totally appalled at her spelling of the word "speaking" here. I love how she knows that I know that she knows how to spell the easy words, thus giving her leave to be lazy.

...it is exactly the same as last year. The girls locker room was re-done and some of the stairwells were painted. Big stinkin' deal. Why don't they save the money they spent on paint and put it towards air conditioning?

By that logic, the school officials could have perhaps sprung for a few extra fans for the second floor in exchange for what they spent on painting the stairwell institutional green. The labor is always cheap, of course. Those Christian school teachers always need the extra dough during the summer months.

You will never believe this in a million years, but for the past couple of mornings, Todd and I have been getting up at 5:15 a.m. to go jogging. Yuck! Anyway we just jog to Kennedy

Ave. and walk back. It's not too terrible. The Hook-meister did his little authoritarian speech today in chapel. His ensemble was completed by his Mother-big set of impressive keys.

Do not forget the Vice Principal of Enforcement's short-sleeved dress shirt and handlebar mustache. Fascism and Fashion may sound alike, but they, unlike us, are not related.

I suppose you didn't happen to catch the Emmy Awards. It was such a joke! The people who pick the winners have no taste. Anyway, they showed Glenn Close sitting in the audience and The Rich-Meister was sitting next to her and he started doing his name thing. You know, 'Glenn, the Glennster, making movies, Senorita Glendita.' She just sat there with this little smile on her face and didn't even laugh. I was dying. My mom just gave me a dirty look and told me to be quiet.

I just want to apologize for the inclusion of that little gem. While I am apologizing, please remember that you, too, at one time, laughed at the Rich-Meister schtick. What passed for comedy in our younger years had not yet evolved enough to reveal to us that Rob Schneider was only capable of making a catch phrase funny for about five minutes.

(This part of the letter was written the day after the beginning. Which was by the way August 28, 1991)

In case I forgot what year it was. I had not, as yet, begun attending the famous Dordt College pit parties, and therefore, at the time of her writing this, still possessed all of my brain cells.

So anyway, just excuse all the stupidness in this stupid letter and go out and find yourself a man. Do it for all of us who are stuck in the black hole of male civilization. "Have a nice day. "Your cousin (duuuuuhhhhhh) "stephanie. (i don't have to capitalize anything, i have creative license, so there!)

Is she making fun of me? I am sure my e.e. cummings phase coincided with my grunge rock phase, so ... yes, she is making fun of me.

P.S. Linda Miller says 'Hi.'

I have absolutely no idea who Linda Miller is. This may be another inside joke that did not stand the test of time, or it could be a peak into Stephanie's random thoughts, which she cannot resist expressing, even on a typewriter with no correction ribbon.

Things would become even more random with the dawn of e-mail, the No. 1 contributor to my many unproductive work days as a small-potatoes reporter in a series of podunk towns over the span of 13 years. Lest you think I am exaggerating, here is a sample e-mail I sent to Stephanie in November of 2006, at my last job:

For your entertainment, here is a list of the things I accomplished at work yesterday:

7:30 a.m. to 8:30 a.m., read a book.

8:30 a.m. to 9 a.m., discussed marriage with Tammy.

9 a.m. to 10 a.m., answered e-mail, made phone calls and did a bit of actual work since Chad the publisher was in the office.

10 a.m. to 10:15, did a little dance when Chad left the office for the day. Discussed with Tammy the latest ep of Lost.

10:15 to 10:30 a.m., sat in Chad's office with Tammy, talking about Chad's new antique office furniture, including two really uncomfortable antique chairs facing his enormous desk, over which now hangs a five-foot wide print of the ugliest, most violent neo-classical Roman battle scene sketch I've ever seen in my life, and talked about how Chad had described it to Tammy: "This is me," (pointing to last guy still astride his horse, guarded by angels) "... and this is everyone else" (pointing to the five hundred Roman soldiers and their horses bleeding to death in the river).

10:30 a.m. to 10:45 a.m., googled name of italian artist responsible for Chad's new horrifying office art, turns out he's very obscure and most websites about him are in Italian. Tammy pointed out that the art was purchased at a flea market disguised as an antique shop, and that there is cockroach poo on the frame. I ask her how she knows what cockroach poo looks like, and she informs me that everyone knows what cockroach poo looks like. Not me, I tell her, because my mom and aunties would have a stroke if they ever saw a cockroach in any of their houses, and we conclude that it's probably a good thing they all grew up in the suburbs and not in Brooklyn.

10:45 a.m. to 11 a.m., More Lost talk.

11 a.m. to 12 noon, had lunch with Erick.

12 noon to 2 p.m., let dog out, played with dog, fed dog, and made a marinade for chicken breasts.

2 p.m. to 3 p.m., back at the office, discussed America's Next Top Model, and other assorted WB programs that David, the sports writer, is forced to watch with his wife, but which he secretly likes, much in the same way that Erick would watch Dawson's Creek with me but denied liking it.

3 p.m. to 3:30 p.m, engaged in a 30 minute Sawyer vs. Jack argument with Tammy. Apparently Tammy likes guys who play head games and who never call you. I tend to prefer men with more attention to hygiene.

Yes, you read correctly. I remain such a slacker that, more than ten years after college, I use work e-mail accounts to write to my friends and relatives about how lazy I am at work. I am getting way ahead of myself. The point is, at the end of my life, will I regret not working hard enough at the office, so that I could become a better reporter and spend 20 more years killing myself and compromising my integrity so I can eventually end up achieving a dream job as a nationally syndicated newspaper columnist at the expense of living life? Or will I regret keeping my stress level to a minimum, and taking the time to make my best friend smile a little bit during her tragically short life? No contest. I will always choose a nice chat over responsibility. As a double cousin, it is my life's work.

The Telephone

My telephone is one of those molded plastic aerodynamic things, its best feature being that it is transparent. A girl can see through its skin into its inner workings, its telephonic liver and spleen. When it rings, a tiny hammer clangs on the bell so fast you can hardly see it move. I have seen this happen before, but not often, because I usually do not sit and stare at the telephone, willing it to ring.

When I first obtained this telephone years ago, I asked my emerging friend Liz to call so I could witness the little telephone guts at work. That was cool. But that was staged, and there was little excitement involved. Not the kind of excitement you have when you're waiting for that boy to call.

I had purchased the telephone at the 1986 Highland Christian School's annual silent and live auction. A restless seventh grader freshly solvent with babysitting cash, I perused the offerings of Footprints watercolors and Gaither Trio concert tickets that vied for my attention from the folding tables that lined the halls of my grade school. It was always weirdly exciting to be at school when it was dark outside, because if you were there at night, it was for something special, and not anything to do with school work.

I saw the see-through telephone in its cardboard box, and I knew I had to have it. Me being a compliant child, I ran to find my dad, begging him to let me bid on the telephone. I had never had my own telephone in my own bedroom before. My father informed me that there was no way I would be able to afford a telephone, and how about I just bid on some dolls or stuffed toys. My bedroom was already packed to the rafters with almost every permutation of Barbie and her related accouterments. I had Care bears and Cabbage Patch dolls. I had a soft teddy bear that looked exactly like Pooky, the bear that belonged to the cartoon cat Garfield, and I had named him the same. At last year's live auction, Dad had bid on and won for me a giant stuffed unicorn. My room was a stuffed toy convention, well into junior high, and dad wanted me to buy more?

It was perhaps my desire for a telephone that was yet another signal to him that I was growing up, which had no doubt occurred to him with the way I was now decorating the walls of my room. The Christopher Reeve-as-Superman posters were now replaced by a prematurely sexed up poster of Kirk Cameron. He had to have been no more than 16 when that random photographer captured him laid out on the cushions in a sleeveless tee and an awkward come-hither stare. That poster was pornography for the preteen set in 1985. In 20 years, I would not blame Kirk one bit for becoming a wackadoodle Left Behinder. What does one do after looking back at a career of acting in what might possibly be the most poorly written sitcoms since the invention of cathode ray tubes? It was either Christian fundamentalism or a life of robbing video stores to support a crack cocaine habit for Kirk.

In that year that brought us "Back to the Future," my fantastical unicorn posters were also gone, replaced by pin-ups of Sean Astin, the Coreys, and worst of all, Duran Duran. This was a sign of bad things to come, at least unto the mind of the good Christian people like my mother and father, who had been alerted by various television preachers to watch out for the phenomenon of fancy-looking English fops who enjoyed yachting. At first it was just one small picture cut out of Seventeen magazine. Then, as the group had gained popularity, more pictures of the mascaraed Simon, John, Nick and Andy were Scotch-taped to the lavender paint of my textured plaster walls. These were entertainers so far outside the universe of the entertainment our family mainly approved of, namely nothing more risque than Tennessee Ernie Ford. But it was Mom and Dad who'd let me have a boombox, so it was just a matter of time before the rock music would infect my Calvinette sensibilities, making me want to shake my buttocks to the beat of whatever was big on the airwaves. Owning a telephone was just another thing to mark the coming of the age 13.

"Fine, go ahead and bid on it, but make sure you don't bid too much. And also I hope you understand that you are not, under any circumstances, getting your own phone line."

I knew better than to ask for that. Although Dad worked for the telephone company and could have had 19 or more phone lines installed for free at our three-bedroom ranch on Indiana Street, with free long distance, such a request had not ever occurred to me. Separate phone lines for teenagers was to the 1980s what a Mom-funded teen credit card was in the 1990s. Not even in the realm of possibility for people like us, a thing we assumed only existed in the movies.

The see-through telephone cost me only $7 of the $21 I had carried with me in my velcro wallet. I placed it on my white lacquered night table, and there it stayed through the remaining months of junior high, into high school and through college, when the Duran Duran pin-ups were replaced by The Cure and R.E.M., and Kirk Cameron was replaced by Johnny Depp and The Beatles.

Today, the telephone is sitting, not ringing, and I am watching it not ring. My wind-up alarm clock, the square one that looks like was time-warped here from the 1950s, with its harsh block numbers and extremely loudly ticking second hand, says the time is eleven minutes to eight. It is not yet time for the call I am expecting.

The sky is dark outside my window, and I get a tiny thrill. I am getting a telephone call from a boy, after dark. This must be what it is like to be on my own, in my own apartment, in my 20s, lying on my bed in my own awesome little room with nothing else to do but field the many telephone calls from adoring men, who call after dark. Someday my life will be like that. Someday my life will be like Audrey Hepburn in "Breakfast At Tiffany's." (At this point in life, I'd only seen the movie and not read the book by Truman Capote, and therefore had no idea that Holly Go-Lightly was essentially a prostitute; I was too distracted by Audrey's fabulous hats.)

I am reclining on my kitten comforter, enjoying the torture of the silence. The build up is awful and awesome.

7:50 p.m. He is not set to call me for another ten minutes. But I have cleared my schedule for the evening. Not that my social calendar overflowed with offers, but I have friends. We spend many Friday nights at basketball games, gossiping and people-watching, then head off to Chili's for more talk and cheap chips and salsa and root beer.

I have told my friends that tonight I am not going to the game, because he is supposed to call. Just saying the words, "He's calling tonight" out loud, made me excited, maybe even more excited than the time he kissed me, which was my first kiss ever, but very obviously was his seventeenth kiss. My friends all seemed fine with the idea of me staying home tonight, a little jealous smirk from one of the twins as she waved back as I headed out to the parking lot. I had the anxious happy butterfly in my stomach all the way home, thinking about him. I tossed my books under my bed as soon as I arrived. Who could do homework at a time like this? At dinner, I said no, I did not want to watch movies with Mom tonight while Dad was out bowling. I left out the details, but Mom seemed fine with reading her novels instead of videos.

I am curled up on my kitten comforter and I am happy. I have nine minutes until I hear his voice. I scoot my fancy pillow down from the headboard and tuck it under my face, the pillow I am technically not supposed to lie on because the shams are the fancy ones with ruffles and they are for show. But I am trying to get comfortable while I gaze at my awesome phone, wondering what we will talk about. I had not thought about what I might say to him. I am still young enough that I never tire of talking about myself, young enough to have no desire to hide anything, enthusiastic enough to engage in any of the topics that frenetically bounce around in my head at all times, because everything right now is important and life-changing and dramatic and meaningful and there is just so much to discuss about everything.

Having my own phone is wonderful. I glance at the clock. Eight minutes left. This horrible alarm clock has been forced upon me, ever since I stopped waking up at the sound of my clock radio. I had it set on WXRT, and the safe-yuppie-progressive music of mostly Talking Heads and The Squeeze would blare in its edgy-yet-not-offensive way that WXRT always does. But after a while, the music just became part of my dreams and I continued to sleep, hazily wondering where David Byrne had indeed left his beautiful wife and house. So now I get to stare at the cheap square cube with hard corners that wakes me up with a sound that makes my tonsils rattle.

But tonight is Friday, and I do not have to set my alarm. I am camped out here, in my fuzzy slippers and jeans and T-shirt, not expecting him to be as early as eight minutes ahead of schedule, but knowing full well that it is perfectly reasonable for a boy to call five minutes early if he is totally in love with you and he has nothing to hide. And if that boy does decide to call early, it is best to be ready to answer, just in case his watch is three minutes fast. I would want to be present and not on the toilet when he calls, and I had taken care of that right after dinner. I would not want him to have to listen to the phone ring five times or more, causing him to think I was even the slightest bit casual about the fact that he was calling. I would want him to know that I was looking forward to talking to him as he was looking forward to talking to me.

Seven minutes. I remember that I am not the only soul in the house with the propensity to answer the telephone should it ring. Mom is in her room with her novel, but she has a phone in there, too.

It is a given that I am much quicker than she, for she is 40 and old, and I am 16 and in love. But I had better make sure I pounce on the phone first. I creak down the hall and knock on her door, which is open slightly.

"Yeah," she answers, not looking up from her book. She is lying diagonally on her and Dad's bed. The ivory polyester bedspread with the single off-center rainbow stripe is still tightly tucked under the pillows. It is 1990 and Mom and Dad still have not burned these bed linens which look as if they have been around since Too Close for Comfort was cancelled. I guess she just takes care of things better than I do, and things last longer. Mom could read there all day and never muss up the bedcovers. Mine always looks as if I have tucked a live grenade under the sheets, pulled the pin, and hid in my sliding-door closet until the smoke cleared.

Mom likes to say my room looks like a tornado hit it, and she does not understand where I get that from. I am sure her friends tell her that it is just a teen thing, that teenagers are messy, but what she does not know is I will never grow out of being a terrible housekeeper and I will forever fail to pick up after myself until the piles of shit around me start to bother me, long after the shit has been bothering other people.

"Mom, if the phone rings, could you let me answer it?"

"Hmm." She is still reading and not looking up. This tells me she has heard me make a noise but she has registered nothing I have said. This happens when she watches TV, too.

"Mom!"

Now she glares. "Wha-at!" She always makes this two syllables when I annoy her.

"If the phone rings, don't answer it, OK?"

"Fine."

In seconds I am belly flopping back on my own bed. Six minutes.

Well, that was easy. Probably she assumes that Liz is going to call. She knows nothing about any boys who might want to talk to me, and fortunately, she cannot read it on my face. The only boys my age that my mother is aware of are the boys from church, with whom I have attended Sunday School since I was in diapers. Boys who have known me my whole life, but who could not tell you a certain thing about me beyond what freaky Robert Smith pictures I have taped up inside my locker at Illiana Christian High School. If any of them ever had any inclination to date me, they never showed it.

But this guy is not like those boys. This boy is not of our people. Not a wooden-shoe-wearing bone in his body, nor is he from our church. He goes to public school. Perhaps attending public school does not necessarily make him and his friends nicer people, but they are worlds away from the doughy boys who torment me at school, with their uptight ways and Weirdo Radar, specifically tuned to pick up the psychic noise made by any girl wearing too much black, or any boy not interested in sports or buying the newest pair of Z-Cavariccis.

Five minutes. My stomach gives a nasty flip. I stare at the phone. If he meant to be early, now would be the time to call. But I have to remind myself. He is not the same as my people, who arrive for everything eons before their time. Walking in to church at fifteen minutes before the service was cutting it close. Twenty minutes is better, to ensure a good seat. Actually arriving at the precise minute you are expected? Inexcusably late. He is not like that. When we get into a relationship, when he is my boyfriend (my stomach lurches again at the notion that this phone call might have behind it the purpose of sorting out how I feel about having a boyfriend), I will need to acclimatize myself to this guy's more laid-back, public school ways of doing things.

After all, he is a sort-of Presbyterian, like Liz, and who knows what time those people arrive at church. Liz is almost always late for everything because she is an artist who is constantly in the middle of projects. Even at 7:30 in the morning when I pick her up for school, she has got oil paint on her face, bed-head and an empty stomach. I wonder if he gets like that, too. Everything about him is an exotic mystery.

Four minutes. Maybe I should have some music in the background. I get up and prance over to my Sanyo stereo and knuckle through my pile of cassette tapes. The Cure would be a good choice. He loves The Cure, and so do I, but "Disintegration" has more of a break-up kind of theme. I would not want him to get the wrong idea. But then again, if he hears me listening to this, then maybe he will learn some things about me. That I am not just friendly and perky but also contemplative and deep. Because that is what I am.

He would like that, because he is deep, also. I know this because one time, at a youth group lock-in at Liz's church, we all talked about the afterlife. Most of us shared some typical Sunday School theories about what might happen after you die. When it seemed like it was my turn, I said I was not sure what happens after a person dies, but I am certain we are not supposed to worry too much about it, and that we are meant to be happy. He seemed to like that answer, and he then proceeded to share his own idea that the universe is made up of many different dimensions, and when we die, we just pass from one dimension to be born into another dimension, where we're reborn and live life all over again but in a way that was totally unrecognizable or even understandable to this world. Our souls just keep getting passed around for infinity from one dimension to the next, and none of it really means anything, it was just that way.

In my head I knew that was a pretty craptastic idea, but I kept that to myself. Because I decided that even if he was nuts, he had obviously spent a lot of time thinking this through, and I respected him for that. And I guess if someone thinks that hard, that makes them pretty deep. Most boys I know spend time thinking about sports and which I.O.U. sweatshirt to go with their ice-washed jeans, and simply regurgitate the Heidelberg Catechism when they need to on Sundays, without really thinking about what they were declaring. Compared to those boys, I will take the crazy one who has no filter.

Three minutes to go, I had better pick the music. Probably it is too soon in our relationship for him to overhear me casually listening to The Cure. One does not casually listen to The Cure, anyway. One Listens to The Cure. Preferably while crying about the fact that one is forced to live in the suburbs. I would have to wait to let him see my darker side. R.E.M. would have to do. He was the one who'd introduced me to them, after all, so if he heard the "Document" album playing in the background, then he would know for sure that I take him seriously, or that I am just so cool that I happen to be listening to this.

The words matter little with R.E.M. when I am 17, which is an added benefit. He'd have no reason to think I was lying here considering suicide while listening to "The Finest Worksong" because nobody could tell what the heck Michael Stipe is singing about. "Document" it is.

Two minutes to go and I am letting the quirky rhythms and strangled vocals of my new favorite band wash over me and my Care Bears. I stretch my legs out in front of me and look down at my fuzzy slippers. Well, this will not do. If I am going to seem confident to him on the phone, I need to feel confident myself. Off come the slippers, on goes the lip gloss. The white T-shirt needs to go, too. He would never, ever be seen wearing white. I tear through my closet and try to find the most appropriate thing to put me in the right seeming mood. What shirt would communicate best via the phone lines that I am eager and nice and friendly, but also deep and interesting. Well, that is an easy choice. Tie-dye. Not just any, but my black and white tie-dye, the one my mother hates. Of course, what was I thinking? A girl must always wear something her mother hates when on the phone with a boy. Had the years of Degrassi taught me nothing?

One minute to go. Gosh, he probably, very emphatically, does not watch Degrassi when he gets home from school. I'd better not bring that up.

I love this music so much. It is crazy sounding. Much crazier than he is, but it is so interesting. I close my eyes for a minute.

Oh crap. I sit bolt upright and open my eyes. It is 8 p.m. and I have not even checked the ringer. Phew. It's on. Any second now.

Geez, this is exciting. What will I say after I hang up the phone, after potentially hours and hours of witty banter and flirtatious laughter and sharing of deep thoughts? Mom will sidle down to my end of the hall to ask me who that was on the phone. Wasn't there as basketball game tonight? Are Liz and the twins not feeling well?

I will just have to make something up, because the phone is about to ring. I position myself so I am staring directly at the silver bell inside the plastic receiver, just so I can watch him wake up my phone. It will be almost like he is in the room with me.

It is now 8:01 p.m. OK, well, maybe his watch is a few minutes slow. I hear a shuffling in the hallway. Mom's coming. She does not knock.

"What are you doing?"

"Nothing."

She pulls a face. "What are you listening to?"

"R.E.M."

"Rem?" she says it like a word instead of letters that stand for something. "As in sleeping?"

"Yes, but no. It's spelled out. Just R.E.M."

"Well they are B.A.D.!" She laughs at her own hilarious joke.

"Mother!"

She collects herself then eyeballs me. "What are you wearing?"

"I changed my shirt."

She is disgusted.

"What? I made this one myself."

She rolls her eyes. "Yeah, I know. You're not leaving the house in that shirt, are you?"

"No mother, I'm waiting for a phone call."

What she does not know is that in a matter of weeks I will be not only wearing this homemade black tie-dyed shirt outside of the house, but I will be pairing it with a set of paratrooper combat boots that I buy myself for my birthday at Army Navy Surplus over in Hammond, despite her begging me to reconsider even as I head out the door with Liz, who is my greatest personal cheerleader.

"Oh, well, hurry it up because I gotta call Bev."

"Haven't you talked to Aunt Bev liked seventeen times already today?”

"Don't be a smart ass. We need to talk about who's having Sunday coffee because it's my turn but I have choir so I will have to be at church early and she might have to bring extra stuff because I won't have time to get it ready before church."

I roll my eyes. "Well, I'm waiting for a phone call and I have no idea when the call is coming but it should be soon and I don't know how long we will be on."

"Don't roll your eyes at me. I'll just call Bev real quick a minute and you can call Liz back when I am done, in case she calls while I'm on the phone."

I sit up. "That's not going to work. I'm supposed to wait."

"She'll understand."

I glance at the alarm clock and sigh. Three minutes after eight. "It's not Liz."

She cocks her head and asks, "The Twins? Joy?" But she already knows it is none of those people.

"It's a boy. That's why I can't call him back, OK?"

"What boy?"

"Just a boy."

"What's his name?"

"He's a guy, OK?"

"Do I know this boy?"

"No, mother."

"I think I have a right to know--"

"Oh geez, do you think this could wait until after my phone call? Then you can call Liz's mom because she knows him and she can tell you all about how he's perfectly nice and stuff." Liz's mother is extremely happy with everyone she meets and I happen to know that she thinks this boy is nothing short of delightful. She is the perfect adult to calm down somebody else's crazy uptight parents about things. I once heard Liz's mom talk about who are we to judge people of another faith, if that faith is sincere and they're not hurting anyone? She has two grown kids who are Baha'i and she still talks to them. That is how cool the Presbyterians are. She will let just about anything fly.

"A boy from Liz's church?"

"Yes, mother, he's Presbyterian and not Christian Reformed so try not to faint."

"Well, I gotta use the phone, so ..."

"Mom, just wait five more minutes." Five minutes past eight now. Even if his watch is slow, it could not be that slow. Now he's just teasing me, I think.

She glares. "Five minutes." She leaves me alone and I roll my eyes to heaven once more for good measure. She drives me nuts when she's in my room.

"And clean up in there, it looks like a tornado came through," she calls from the other end of the hall.

What if something happened to him? Five more minutes is not nearly enough of a grace period if he has fallen off his skateboard and injured himself. What if he has been taken to the emergency room right now? Well, if he is in the emergency room, then he's probably not going to call until way later, like 10 p.m., and I have very little upbeat yet thoughtful music in here to keep me entertained until then.

What the heck is Stipe singing about anyway?

8:06 p.m. In life, a person can get away with being five minutes late for anything. Five minutes late for class, you might be able to squeak by if you have a cool teacher. Six minutes late, forget about it, unless you're on the soccer team and your next class is English as taught by Mr. Cole, your coach. Well, this guy is most certainly not on a soccer team, and most definitely not a jock of any kind, and therefore has no excuse as a jock who can successfully beg forgiveness for his unfounded sense of entitlement instilled by the adults in his life who live vicariously through him. So, what's *his* excuse?

At 8:07 p.m., I close my eyes and pray. God, if you make him call me right now, I promise I will memorize my catechism for the rest of the year, even though the catechism teaches that we may not bargain with you. I personally believe you are open to suggestions because really, you and I know each other pretty well. So what do you say?

The next moment I am startled by a small clang, and for a brief second I think the phone is indeed ringing. I pop my eyes open and sit up, gasping for breath. But no. I have only fallen asleep on my bed and my hand has limply fallen on the receiver, causing the tiny hammer thing to ring the bell for a lame half second. It is now 8:10 p.m.

Something happens then. I am staring, still, at the unringing phone. I begin to doubt that he is injured, and I am beginning to doubt myself. For the first time I wonder if he's going to call before 9 p.m. He said he would call at eight. Who says he is going to call at a certain time and then does not? Who?

Why did I change my shirt to talk on the phone? Who does that?

Mom is at the door again. I speak first. "Go ahead."

She goes away and I hear her pick up the extension in the kitchen, automatically dialing the seven worn off numbers that belong to her sister. I hear her speaking but I cannot make out what she is saying, and I close my eyes again. I stay awake this time. Instead I wonder if it is too late to make plans, and if the girls would even want to make plans with me after I begged off the basketball game for a phone call from a boy who might or might not even be interested in me. And was she jealous, or was that smirk about something else?

What was the point of any of this? I am a desirable, young, attractive girl who might be a size 12 but I do get checked out by plenty of unknown guys who have not watched me fail to memorize my catechism every single Sunday since birth. Why should I waste my time waiting for this one guy to call me? I could be getting phone calls from half a dozen guys every night if I were more of a flirt.

Mom has hung up now. I sigh. If he calls, he calls. If not, so what.

I hop off the bed and stop the tape. I push the On button for the record player on the stereo and remove a black disk from a large red cardboard jacket that is the soundtrack for the Broadway musical "Annie," featuring Andrea McArdle, a girl I wanted to be just five years earlier.

I flop back on the bed and sprawl out on my back, closing my eyes and mouthing the words along with the ragamuffin cast of little girls singing "It's a Hard Knock Life." I remember how my former friend Tracy and I used to argue when she stupidly insisted that the girls were singing "It's a Hard Enough Life," even after I'd shown her the record jacket with the title of the song. The words were right in front of her but she was determined to sing "enough" every time they sang "knock," claiming that she'd never heard of the phrase "hard knock."

Tracy never appreciated it when I would correct her on things like that, especially when it came to song lyrics. Probably because it happened so often, because she was always getting it wrong and I have an excellent ear.

As I lie there I also remember that when I was much smaller in size and stature, I used to climb on top of my dresser and stare out the bedroom window whenever Annie began singing "Maybe." I would stare out onto the quiet cul-de-sac at my dad's cream Chevy Nova which had a permanently reclining passenger seat being held in place by cinder blocks, and I would wonder when my own Daddy Warbucks was coming to take me to his mansion in Manhattan in his Bentley. I do not really want to leave, though. That bald Albert Finney scared me a little bit. Even when my own Dad shaved off his mustache, I was scared of him for at least a week.

I roll over and open my eyes. I train my stare on that ugly little telephone, and I wonder if I have the spunk and the will to make things go my way, like Annie. Sometimes if I will it hard enough, things do happen. Like sometimes, when I think about picking up the phone to call Liz, somehow she is already calling me. More than once we have called each other at the exact same time, and were instantly connected when I picked up to dial.

Maybe he and I could have that kind of connection. I hope so. So I stare and stare, and I think.

Ring, little hammer and bell.

If he does not call, then somebody please call. Ring already. Work, little telephone liver and spleen.

Vibrate. Wiggle. Live.

Ring.

Ring.

Ring.

Fairy Godmother

Sometime after my second Shiner Bock I realize I am watching three-year-old boys scream over my godson's new toy workbench with its puffy plastic hammer and cartoonishly big bolts, and it occurs to me that I have no business being here. And then I crack open a third beer.

It is strange that I should feel so uncomfortable in my friends' house, the same house around which I have been known to traipse in nothing but a towel and a swim suit. A swim suit I hate because it is a hand-me-down from a formerly chubby former friend, but I wear it because I hate shopping for swim suits even more than I hate this particular swim suit. Aside from my own house and those of close family members, the home in the Stonebridge Ranch neighborhood of McKinney, Texas is the only house where I can help myself to the fridge.

The comfort I have in my friends' home is imposed upon whenever one of Seth and Rachel's two kids age another year. Because that means it is time for that most necessary social obligation: The Toddler Birthday Party.

I am convinced there was a time when parents never bothered to lick stamps just to invite friends and family over to watch a tiny person open gifts. Either times have changed, or the location is to blame. Our friends do not conform to most of the social norms of the 75070 ZIP code: they play Dungeons and Dragons, do not get too bent out of shape when the minivan gets scratched, and Dad spends almost as much time at home with the kids as Mom does. They live in a town where they are surrounded by tiny, bleached blonde women with husbands in a perpetual state of being away on business, forcing their wives to find day care so they can spend their "Stay-At-Home" Mom years at Lifetime Fitness and the Korean nail salon in order to keep the flames of passion alive once the husband does make an appearance. These women can be identified by possessions and attributes that are fashionably too large for their petite frames: Escalades, Harry-Carey-inspired Gucci sunglasses, and augmented ta-tas as hard as their abs. Somehow, the UV rays and silicone have affected their maternal chromosomes, implanting the desire, no, the NEED, to throw lavish birthday parties for people who are in diapers, who have the attention span of puppies, and who would rather play with pots and pans than sit still long enough to open, one by one, a hundred or more high-dollar presents, and to pause after each one so mommy can snap a picture for her Creative Memories photo album. Our dear friends are not these people.

Still, the pressure to party McKinney style is there. And I and my husband go to these parties because we love our friends, we love buying presents, and because Caleb, age 3, and Kayla, age 5, are two of the most delightful little people in our lives, and because I love being Caleb's fairy godmother. Yes, that is my own lame nickname for myself.

In effect, Kayla is also our goddaughter. In Caleb's case, we took the vow at the front of church at his baptism, witnessed by the congregation and the whole shebang. For Kayla, another couple took the vow. We will call them Lauren and Jim. I may as well, because they are around so seldom that I can hardly recall their actual names. If I sound judgmental, I am. I do not pretend not to be. In fact, I fully embrace my hypercritical attitude, and I do not apologize for it. It may make me appear overwrought, but I am quite serious about things we say out loud in front of God and his people. And besides, being judgmental gives me endless things to write about. So anyway, after Kayla was baptized, Lauren and Jim all but disappeared. Not as in abducted-by-a-UFO disappeared. They are a childless couple who live 20 miles away and got tired of Seth and Rachel turning them down for social outings "because of the baby." My husband and I also are childless and lived 20 miles away at the time, but unlike Lauren and Jim, we waited it out. We rarely planned elaborate outings, knowing that finding a babysitter makes everything more complicated and expensive.

So in that first year after Kayla was born, Erick and I gave them their space, and then casually started to mosey over to the house, hanging out on the sofa and watching Trading Spaces with our exhausted friends. Pretty soon, it was the five of us and Kayla, and eventually Caleb, hanging out on weekends around the pool or inside playing Mah Jongg.

Because we became so involved in their lives, we ended up becoming the default godparents of Kayla. If we bought Caleb a picture Bible for his baptism anniversary, we'd buy something age-appropriate for Kayla. You cannot give a kid a present on a spiritual milestone and and not give one to his sister. Especially when that sister is under the age of 5. It just would not do. This also means we have to muddle our way through parties sponsored by Mattel.

For Kayla's age 3 birthday gift, Erick and I eschewed the Barbie doll theme implied by the mailed invitation. Instead, we bought her a book called "Alice the Fairy," about a little blonde girl with springy, crazy curls, who lives in her head and pretends to make things appear and disappear with her magic wand. The best part is, she hates broccoli. I myself enjoy broccoli, but the book is justified because it is wonderfully subversive, especially in today's atmosphere of school board members freaking out on the evening news at least once a week, yammering about how all our children are obese and they are going to get diabetes if we give them a bite out of a single Chips Ahoy cookie.

I was very, very proud of having found this book. I did not even mind so much that Lauren showed up to the party, seemingly out of the blue. And I especially did not care that all of Kayla's other presents, purchased for her mostly by people I saw only at these birthday parties, were Barbie dolls. As she opened one pink box after another in her parents' living room, surrounded by politely interested adults and bored children, I assured myself that one day all those Barbie dolls will look exactly the way mine look today: frazzled with weirdly sticky hair, and faces with a strange, pinkish hue from all the time I spent trying to apply my mother's makeup on them. On the other hand, books last forever. FOREVER, I smugly told myself as my darling Kayla, she of the shy smile and devastating blue eyes, opened up a box bigger than herself – indeed, a box into which she could retire if she ever were to become a homeless toddler – to find her much-desired Barbie scooter. "Oh wow!" "Oh my!" "How fun!" Hold up gift. Smile. Click. It was not unlike attending a bridal shower, except with a lot of crying rug rats and grown men who sold insurance during the week but were today wearing deconstructed cargo shorts and were exhibiting more interest in picking at the corners of their beer bottle labels.

"Alice the Fairy" did not get quite the same reception as the scooter. But that was OK. The book was for Kayla, and not for the eerily quiet adults at the party, who were on the verge of pulling a muscle as they craned their necks to see if there was a real gift accompanying the book. Due to the many times that Erick and I had babysat for our friends, we both were secure in the knowledge that Kayla loves to read, and to be read to. Aside from the grandparents, I wondered how many of these people had offered to babysit the two children so Seth and Rachel could go out to dinner and then make out like teenagers on a darkened country road in their Cheerio-encrusted Honda Odyssey. Anyone? Anyone? Hands? I did not think so. Igniting the flame of passion in exhausted parents of two toddlers must surely earn me a whopper of a Calvinette badge. Probably from a more liberal church in Grand Rapids somewhere.

While we adults all watched the ceremonial opening of the presents, I began to hear whispers about the cake. I thought little of it until I wandered into the kitchen toward the laundry room to grab another Shiner. And there it was. I am not one of those feminists who hate Barbie because of the poor body image she imposes on little girls. I am certainly a feminist, just not that kind. I was that kind of feminist in college, but then I got over it when a highly educated and enlightened woman named Gretchen told me that Barbie dolls actually help little girls develop their fine motor skills. Don't believe it? Try pulling on a pair of gold hot pants over those bendable plastic legs, millimeter by millimeter, and you will get the idea. There was something very wrong with the Barbie doll on that particular day, on this particular cake. It seemed Barbie had gone on a bender and ran away with the circus, spending a lost weekend as the beautiful assistant to a Ken-sized magician David Copperfield doll whose tiny illusionist's hacksaw trick had gone awry and sliced poor Barbie completely in half.

From the waist up, she looked fine. She sat smiling, frozen in a waving pose from atop the cake, which had been molded in the shape of a giant "Gone With the Wind" style hoop skirt. Because, really, you cannot get enough to eat out of a sheath dress cake, or even a mermaid-style gown cake. The location of her legs was a mystery, and I was praying that nobody asked that questioned out loud, and nobody ate enough cake to reach the middle of it, to reveal the legless wonder, lest somebody be forced to explain to the 3-year-old birthday girl that the procedure did not hurt when Barbie's ass got chopped off. The overall effect was cute, I guess. But the other adult guests were over the moon about this Barbie cake.

"Does anybody know who made this?"somebody asked. Just to avoid protracting the issue any further in case you had not guessed already, the creator of this mutilated toy/pastry combo was Lauren. As soon as word got around, all conversation was about Lauren.

"Isn't she talented?"

"Isn't that clever?"

"Who is she?"

"Oh, she's the godmother."

In reality, I was mutely, politely, consuming a slice of the skirt cake. In my mind, I was in the corner knocking my head against the wall. I had many wicked and ungenerous thoughts about Lauren that day, most of which were along the lines of: I hope she knows that a BARBIE DOLL CAKE does not count toward her godmother deficit, as it has nothing to do with the child's spiritual upbringing, unless sawed-off Barbie was risen from the dead and I did not get the memo.

But I was raised right. I never say any of those horrible things out loud. Instead, I just popped open another Shiner.

The whole idea rubs me wrong because my people do not do toddler birthday parties, generally. Some of us throw a party for the one-year-old kid, just to take the obligatory photograph of the child sitting in the high chair with smashed chocolate cake all over her face. I myself, at the age of 1, chose to partake in an after-cake banana, according to the evidence in my mother's photo albums. Today, there are so, SO, many first cousins with about 18 kids apiece, these celebrations generally end up being a party involving only the child's mother, father, brothers, sisters and grandparents.

When I was in elementary school, and one of my classmates threw a birthday party, there were no written invitations. Somebody announced it at school, and everybody was invited. I would get dropped off at a kid's house, where that kid's mother – with maybe the help of a sister or a friend, if she was a nervous and soft-spoken type, but so few of the women amongst our people are quite that incompetent – would sit us down at the dining room table to finger-paint, and then we would watch that kid open presents until that got boring, and then we'd have cake and ice cream, and then the mommies and daddies would come back and pick us all up and we'd go home. Bing, bang, boom.

Now, at least in the swankier suburbs, where the mothers have more access to money than to drill sergeant skills, they hire train conductors. Yes, my dear, sweet friend Rachel, a beautiful Southern belle who often gets understandably overwhelmed by the pressures of being a good mother, even though she is already a great mother in her own right, hired a train conductor to bring his miniature train to Saddle Club Lane for Caleb's second birthday. When she told me this and I hung up the phone, I turned to Erick and said, "Is that child going to look back and remember his big train ride birthday?" Erick, who is much nicer than I am and who never criticizes anybody out loud, just shook his head.

"I'll tell you the answer to that! No! He's not going to remember any of it! He's going to ride on a pretend train around his pretend neighborhood, and then he's going to come back and open all his expensive gifts, go play with an old sock, have some cake, poop in his pants and take a nap." Erick just looked at me like he was sad that so many things get on my nerves. He has that expression a lot. The year of the train theme, the pressures of the suburbs got the best of us, and we sprung for the big guns. A big, toy workbench, fit for a minimum age group slightly older than the boy.

They say if you hate the weather in Texas, wait five minutes and it will change. That winter day, it changed with a vengeance into a freezing wind, and the train conductor canceled. My ever-prepared friend had a back up plan. Gingerbread houses.

I have to say here that Rachel's gingerbread house idea was a much better plan than mine and Stephanie's, those many years ago. Rachel bought kits. The from-scratch variety continues, in my mind, to look like fun. Sort of in the same way that communal living is an excellent idea on paper, but in practice people just plain get on each other's nerves. In the Great Gingerbread Debacle of '95, nerves were indeed gotten upon. Back then, I had had no idea there were things called pre-made kits. I'd like to think if we had taken that route back in '95, the whole thing would have taken the four cousins about an hour, and then we could have just pretended to still be busy when the mothers telephoned us to alert us that we were due for night church, and then spent the afternoon watching terrible movies on the console television in my parents' basement.

Upon arrival to Caleb's party and discovering the loss of the train ride activity, Erick and I were promptly assigned to a team of toddlers to help build their own houses to take home. I was teamed up with Kayla and one of her little friends from down the street. Me having no desire to pretend to be a teacher or a leader of any sort, I was pretty much down with whatever the little chickies wanted to do. Gum drops on the windows? Sure! Peppermint sticks squashed on the front lawn? Excellent. Fifteen snowman cookies glued to the roof? Well, clearly a violation of building codes, but then again, why not? I will tell you why not -- because the rest of the teams had been completely railroaded by their adult supervisors, who were meticulously reproducing the photo on the cover of the box that the gingerbread kits came in. I conspiratorially told my two helpers that "Our gingerbread house is the best one," and saw that Kayla and her little friend were beyond pleased to know it.

Alas, I was rewarded for trying to build up their self-esteem by being told by another adult, who had overheard my comment, that, "Everyone's house is the best one."

I pondered this conundrum as I looked up from our magnificent Da-Da-esque creation, only to see the gaggle of ankle-biters biting on candy, clearly bored of watching Moms and Dads reinforce the roof with more spackle frosting and following up with painstaking swabs to remove any unsightly spots of white.

One of the mothers was still working on "her son's" gingerbread house when Caleb was halfway through tearing open the gifts.

This day, I was happy to haul myself into the living room to watch the gift opening ceremonies, as I could not wait for Caleb to see his new tools. Caleb stared at the box for a second, and then waited for instructions to move on to the next gift.

However, it was the adults, for once, who were impressed.

"That is so cool. Whose gift was that?" marveled the perfect- gingerbread-house makers.

Erick and I made no announcements. The slightly balding man in the cargo shorts and Abercrombie and Fitch baseball cap did not need to know it was we who bought the best gift. I drank my Shiner and glowed in self satisfaction. The screaming toddlers were konking each other with giant plastic hammers and wrenches because of us. We were the humble champions. We are the godparents.

Postcards From a Dream

Monday night. I cannot sleep. I flip off the TV and shuffle to the kitchen to make some lavender tea. On my way, I hear a "boop" from the office. I check on it. The IM application on my iMac has sprung to life. There's a message to me, Calvinette, from Red-headed Girly-Girl.

RHGG: You called me?

Calvinette: I did.

RHGG: Everything OK?

Calvinette: No. Everything sucks.

RGHH: (Silence)

Calvinette: I wasn't trying to sound angry at you. Just answering honestly.

RHGG: I know. Just that vulgar stuff like "sucks" can startle me now.

Calvinette: Weird. I guess we should switch IM handles. Or maybe you could just take mine and I can be Guttermouth.

RHGG: Hee.

Calvinette: Glad you have your sense of humor.

RHGG: Oh, totally. You wouldn't believe how many hilarious people there are up here.

Calvinette: You being one of them.

RHGG: Thanks!

Calvinette: So what were you doing when I called before?

RHGG: Oh, you know. We're not allowed to talk much about heaven to the living, but I can tell you it's fabulous.

Calvinette: Cool.

RHGG: What are you up to?

Calvinette: Watching How I Met Your Mother.

RHGG: Nice. Good one?

Calvinette: Yeah. They played "You're the Inspiration" from the Chicago 17 album. That's why I called. It was the best episode of HIMYM ever. I wanted to make sure you were watching and then I remembered.

RHGG: That happens. I get that a lot.

Calvinette: So, you can, like, hear it when people make that mistake?

RHGG: Kind of. It's hard to explain, but yes, in a way, I hear it. And not just calling on the phone. Even more I hear those split seconds of thinking about calling me and then the remembering a second later ...

Calvinette: It sucks. But in a way it's cool that you know about it.

RHGG: Yeah.

Calvinette: 'Scool that you can still IM with me, though.

RHGG: It's a new thing they're trying.

Calvinette: Hm. So, in heaven? Who is the "they"? Down here, we always say "they" when we're talking about junk like the cable company or the people who write the dictionary. Who is your "they"?

RHGG: Well ...

Calvinette: I get it. Hard to explain, right?

RHGG: I'm sorry.

Calvinette: No, I'm not mad. I meant for the tone to be more gentle than that. It's the curse of the curmudgeons who hate emoticons. I just meant, I understand that part of it. I'm sure if you get too 'splainy about the afterlife stuff and heaven, or start giving me answers to why Tilda Swinton appears to hate her own perfect figure and insists on wearing potato sacks to the Oscars, my head will explode. Right?

RHGG: Again, sorry to be so vague, but kind of like that, yes. I'm making heaven sounds as if it's turned me into a dullard.

Calvinette: I don't think so. More like Galadriel.

RHGG: Like a crazy beautiful elf queen?

Calvinette: Uh ...

RHGG: What?

Calvinette: That's the first time EVER you've understood a Lord of the Rings reference.

RHGG: Oh.

Calvinette: I'm impressed.

RHGG: Good.

Calvinette: Everything still sucks, though.

RHGG: (Silence)

Calvinette: I'm glad I still get to talk to you, though. Even on IM.

RHGG: For a while.

Calvinette: Do you get to watch HIMYM in Heaven?

RHGG: I could if I wanted to, but I don't really want to. There's so much more stuff to do here that's so much more fun.

Calvinette: More fun that sitting on the sofa in your comfy pants watching Neil Patrick Harris and eating peanut M&Ms?

RHGG: For one thing, it's so green here. You know how in The Sound of Music when Julie Andrews is twirling in the Austrian mountains and it's spectacular and wild and green?

Calvinette: Yes.

RHGG: Doesn't even come close.

Calvinette: Hee.

RHGG: What?

Calvinette: You like the outdoors now?

RHGG: Everything's outdoors.

Calvinette: Ha.

RHGG: I know what you are thinking.

Calvinette: Yes, of course you do because you have the powers of an elven queen now. So then you remember the e-mail you sent me when the two of you first started dating ...

RHGG: Stop it.

Calvinette: And he invited you over to his house to help pull weeds and you said "I don't do yard work. Not for any man."

RGHH: Sigh. Yes, I remember.

Calvinette: HA! You like the outdoors now. You like it outside even more than I do.

RHGG: There are no weeds to pull here.

Calvinette: And I assume you don't have to sit on wet grass to watch the harp concerts?

RHGG: No.

Calvinette: And there are no bugs buzzing around your halo?

RHGG: Indeed, no.

Calvinette: Hmm. I always thought heaven would become the thing that exemplified your purest self. Like, I would imagine that Steve Irwin is up there swimming with the great white sharks and stingrays, all happy in an endless ocean with no stingers or sharp teeth, but the creatures are just ornery enough to offer a satisfying wrestling match once in a while.

RHGG: It is our purest selves. I like that notion. But I haven't met Steve Irwin yet, so I couldn't tell you.

Calvinette: OK, well. I guess I would have thought your perfect heaven would be a giant spa with white marble arches where you wake up every morning getting a scalp massage from Paul Newman.

RHGG: Did you know he's like 30 years old here? He might be prettier than I am. And I have to say, I do look mighty foxy up here.

Calvinette: There it is!

RHGG: Huh?

Calvinette: Now I know for sure it's you.

RHGG: Oh, right.

Calvinette: And can I just say that I am SO TOTALLY jealous that you have now met Paul Newman???

RHGG: I think you just did.

Calvinette: So what other celebrity sightings can you tell me about?

RHGG: Well ...

Calvinette: I know, you're going to tell me that there are no celebrities in heaven because everybody is appreciated and adored equally but not excessively because everybody's mostly into giving praise and adoration to the Big Guy, right?

RHGG: Something like that.

Calvinette: Sounds like heaven's a communist dictatorship.

RHGG: A benevolent one, but yes. And not with sad looking people and bread lines.

Calvinette: Or concrete walls.

RHGG: Or bomb testing.

Calvinette: Or propaganda posters.

RHGG: Or state-sponsored news organizations.

Calvinette: And lots of places to rollerskate.

RHGG: Have you gone yet?

Calvinette: What?

RHGG: Rollerskating.

Calvinette: No, but it's funny you bring it up.

RHGG: Not really. You've been wanting to go do that for a while now.

Calvinette: How did you know that?

RHGG: (Silence)

Calvinette: Oh, yes. Mind-reading elven queen.

RHGG: Anyway, you should go.

Calvinette: Rollerskating?

RHGG: You've been talking about it ever since the week after my funeral.

Calvinette: When I found the knitting pattern for the leg warmers, right?

RHGG: Sort of. And it's been in the back of your head since you saw "Roll Bounce."

Calvinette: That was about three years ago. You can see that far back in my head?

RHGG: In everybody's head. We all can hear everybody's prayers.

Calvinette: Um, excuse me, but I never prayed about rollerskating.

RHGG: Thinking, praying. Same thing.

Calvinette: Every time I think about a Wendy's Frosty, I'm actually asking God to get me one?

RHGG: Out loud, not out loud. To yourself, to God, to your spouse, boss or toll booth attendant. It's all the same, and it's all within earshot.

Calvinette: It must be overwhelming.

RHGG: You would think so, but, again. Heaven and all. Everything just is. The concept of too much doesn't exist. If it was too much, it would be uncomfortable and that would make it antithetical to heaven.

Calvinette: I think I get it. What about–

RHGG: Before you say anything else, I don't really have much else to say about heaven, but if you want to pursue it, I'll do my best.

Calvinette: What you are really trying to say is you don't want to talk about heaven anymore. Heaven sure has made you polite.

RHGG: It's just that I want to talk more about you.

Calvinette: Me? I'm sad. I'm bored. Life is not as fun without you here.

RHGG: I've been hearing that from everyone.

Calvinette: It's true. You were the central figure in a lot of fun memories.

RHGG: You all gave me a fun life. I was very lucky.

Calvinette: Until about a year ago.

RHGG: I'm sorry you had to see me that way.

Calvinette: I wish you would stop being so sorry. You were never that apologetic before.

RHGG: It is what it is.

Calvinette: And you were never so zen either.

RHGG: We do a lot of yoga here.

Calvinette: Hee.

RHGG: What?

Calvinette: Stephanie. Does yoga. Outside on the grass with the ants.

RHGG: All right. It's funny.

Calvinette: Are you really bendy and athletic now?

RHGG: Is that really what you want to ask me?

Calvinette: I guess I already know the answer to that one. OK, so the end. Yes, it was hard seeing you like that. When I first walked in your bedroom – did you know that was the first time I'd seen your bedroom since you moved? I liked it, by the way. The greens and the browns. The scrollwork. Everything was beautiful. Everything felt strangely sacred. I was at least glad that you got to be at home.

RHGG: Me too.

Calvinette: When I first walked in, you were lying on your side and Kim was on the bed next to you, holding your hand. You looked like somebody who had just run a marathon. You looked extremely tired. Just wiped out.

RHGG: I was.

Calvinette: Your hair was starting to come back. That made me really angry inside.

RHGG: Why?

Calvinette: Because the reason your hair had started coming back was because you had to stop taking the chemo, because the chemo wasn't working anymore. And just so we're clear: You were beautiful with hair, without hair, whatever. But the irony of the hair – it just made me so angry. Could you see me?

RHGG: I could see the shape of you.

Calvinette: Could you hear me?

RHGG: Yes.

Calvinette: Do you know what I was thinking even when I was sitting there holding your hand?

RHGG: Yes, but I'd like you to say it out loud.

Calvinette: But I'm not out loud, I'm typing.

RHGG: All the same here.

Calvinette: I was thinking that any minute, Healthy Stephanie was going to sit up and say, "Would everyone please stop holding my hand because it's just a little queer."

RHGG: I'm glad you had a little speck of humor that day.

Calvinette: You always made me laugh the most.

RHGG: Statistically speaking, you made me laugh more often than I made you laugh.

Calvinette: How would you even know that?

RHGG: Um ...

Calvinette: Never mind. So, did you go straight to heaven?

RHGG: I didn't really seem to go anywhere. It sort of feels like I've always been here.

Calvinette: I wish you were still here.

RHGG: I'm here now.

Calvinette: But not really.

RHGG: (Silence)

Calvinette: Were you in pain?

RHGG: When?

Calvinette: You know when.

RHGG: The drugs took care of that. Mostly I was worried about him. And my parents, and Kim, and Todd, and you, and everybody.

Calvinette: I was so worried that you were in pain. At one point, we were watching TV, and he was sitting next to you on the bed and he looked over at you, and you had a tear coming down your cheek.

RHGG: I don't tell you this to disturb you. But I had finally realized that I was going to have to let go. My sensations were going away little by little.

Calvinette: It didn't hurt?

RHGG: I was just having a breakthrough, and it was really hard. But that's over now.

Calvinette: Like going to the dentist? It was bad, you'd rather not dwell on it, but you made it through?

RHGG: Exactly. (eye roll) Death is exactly like going to the dentist.

Calvinette: Or going to the dentist is like dying?

RHGG: Speaking of, you need to go to the dentist.

Calvinette: Why are you being so bossy? "Go rollerskating. Go to the dentist."

RHGG: Because you need someone to boss you. Erick's not going to.

Calvinette: No, he's not. We took that part out of the vows.

RHGG: Right. But seriously, listen. You also need to get your passport already.

Calvinette: Yes.

RHGG: And finish that novel. Any novel. Just finish one.

Calvinette: I'm sorry I didn't finish one before you died.

RHGG: It's fine. I wasn't expecting it. You were always such a slacker.

Calvinette: Will you be able to read it once I do finish it?

RHGG: I'm reading it already.

Calvinette: How embarrassing. The first draft is so carppy.

RHGG: Doesn't matter. I can read the final draft, too.

Calvinette: And?

RHGG: Do you really want to know my opinion?

Calvinette: Yes!

RHGG: Because it doesn't really matter what I think. I'm not the one who's going to publish it.

Calvinette: No, but your opinion matters to me, you know that.

RHGG: Then my opinion is you have work to do before you go on to try to get that one published. You need to work on that collection of short stories. You do that so much better.

Calvinette: But how do I publish that?

RHGG: That will take care of itself.

Calvinette: That doesn't make me any less anxious.

RHGG: But you wanted my opinion.

Calvinette: I guess I can count that as my postcard from heaven.

RHGG: Like Mr. Boerman used to say?

Calvinette: Exactly. By the way, I wish we could have watched the inauguration together. And the premiere of Lost.

RHGG: I would have loved that.

Calvinette: I also wish we could have watched the Oscars together, too.

RHGG: It was a good one.

Calvinette: You saw it?

RHGG: I and everybody I know.

Calvinette: At least you get to have Oscar parties in heaven. So it's sort of still you, exemplified. Hey, I still have your awesome Oscar night margarita recipe. I made it all pretty and I put it in my special family cookbook.

RHGG: Aw. Thanks.

Calvinette: You're welcome.

RHGG: That's another thing. It's going to be your job to bring back "you're welcome."

Calvinette: Meaning ...

RHGG: Haven't you ever noticed that so many times when Person A says "Thank you" to Person B, then Person B says "Thank YOU." Especially in interviews on the radio. "Thank you for coming on the show, Joaquin." "Oh, well, thank YOU, Dave."

Calvinette: I don't think anyone anywhere will be hearing THAT precise exchange anytime soon. But I know what you mean.

RHGG: Good.

Calvinette: So, my job is to bring back "you're welcome."

RHGG: It is a worthy trend.

Calvinette: Anything else?

RHGG: OK, you need to get your shit together already and adopt a kid or two.

Calvinette: ?

RHGG: What?

Calvinette: Shit?

RHGG: I'm allowed one swear.

Calvinette: What???

RHGG: Sigh. I am allowed one swear in my chats.

Calvinette: Is that per day, per week, or what?

RHGG: Just one.

Calvinette: One for all of eternity? Forever and ever amen?

RHGG: Yes.

Calvinette: And you chose THAT moment to say it?

RHGG: The purpose of one swear for all of eternity is to convey something of the utmost importance with a little bit of shock thrown in. I hope it worked.

Calvinette: It did, a little.

RHGG: Perhaps I should have saved it.

Calvinette: No, I get it.

RHGG: Good. Because you really need to get on this adoption thing.

Calvinette: Loud and clear. Anything else?

RHGG: Isn't that enough for one homework assignment?

Calvinette: Am I being graded?

RHGG: By the universe? Yes.

Calvinette: How am I doing?

RHGG: Not so hot, my friend.

Calvinette: Great.

RHGG: Well, I have to go.

Calvinette: Have to? Got an appointment?

RHGG: A scalp massage with Paul Newman.

Calvinette: Funny!

RHGG: A lot of prayers coming in. Just so you know, even when you're not on speaking terms with God, he's still listening. He hears you even when you think you're giving him the silent treatment.

Calvinette: Kind of like a nosy older brother?

RHGG: Mmm, maybe a benevolent nosy older brother.

Calvinette: So I guess I'm getting the exclusive from beyond the grave. God is indeed a good guy.

RHGG: The goodest.

Calvinette: Sigh.

RHGG: Why sigh?

Calvinette: I don't know.

RHGG: You don't have to feel guilty about it.

Calvinette: About what?

RHGG: About being angry at God. He understands.

Calvinette: Well, if he's so benevolent and all knowing and all understanding, then why

RHGG: Don't ask that.

Calvinette: Why not?

RHGG: Everybody who ever has contact with the beyond always wants to know why God lets bad things happen to people who love him, or to people who don't deserve it. Just don't waste your breath. The answer is not as compelling as you might think.

Calvinette: But it's a legitimate question.

RHGG: It is. The question of the ages.

Calvinette: Then ...

RHGG: Just don't.

Calvinette: Fine.

RHGG: Well, like I said, we're pretty busy cataloging the prayers up here so I do have to go.

Calvinette: Sounds like work.

RHGG: It's not work. It's fun.

Calvinette: Because it wouldn't be heaven if it wasn't fun.

RHGG: Sarcasm isn't going to make you feel any better.

Calvinette: Maybe I'm not ready to feel better.

RHGG: No. I suppose you're not. Neither is he.

Calvinette: I know.

RHGG: Take care of yourself.

Calvinette: Bye.

I sign off and head to the kitchen to continue making my tea. It comes out of the microwave steaming, and I add a little splash of honey and lemon, and a finger or two of whiskey. I stand at the counter and make a list with a Sharpie on a Post-It pad that I leave on the counter for phone messages and instructions from the spirit world:

- Go rollerskating
- Make dentist appointment
- Apply for passport
- Finish novel
- Finish short story collection
- Adopt a kid already
- Bring back you're welcome
- Don't feel guilty about the God question.

Epilogue

The following is a letter I wrote to President Obama a week before he was set to take office. I am still waiting for a reply. This text has not been edited for its inclusion in this book, and as you can see, I was still having a hard time referring to my cousin in the past tense consistently. Also, at the time I wrote this, I was not equipped with all the facts of early detection of uterine cancer. I encourage you to do your own research, and, most importantly, speak to your doctors and family members about possible genetic risk factors and symptoms.

Dear President-Elect Barack Obama,

I'd like to tell you about my best friend, Stephanie, of Lansing, Illinois, who left this earth on New Year's Eve, 2008, after a seven month battle with endometrial uterine cancer.

She was 32, had recently passed the Illinois Bar after completing law school at Chicago Kent University. Her story is even more tragic in that on December 1, she celebrated her one-year wedding anniversary with her husband and her true love, Dan.

Stephanie and Dan worked on our high school newspaper together back in the 1990s, and in 2006, the two of them bumped into each other at a White Sox game. Separately, they are two of the wittiest, funniest and smartest people I know. Together, they could hold court at any family gathering without even having to try.

I grew up an only child in a huge extended family, and Stephanie was like a sister to me. Our families did everything together when we were kids. She was the Lucy to my Ethel, and the Louise to my Thelma.

She voted for you, and she was so excited to see you take office. She and I never got the chance to do a lot of things together, and watching your inauguration and your presidency unfold were among those things. I'm at least grateful that in the midst of her 30 rounds of intense chemotherapy, she had the energy to go to the polls.

The grief rippling through our families is indescribable. But we also have joyful memories of her life, which she lived fully. Our families are comprised of some of the most staunchly blue collar Republicans you'll ever meet. Stephanie and I were the exceptions to that rule. As we came of age during the Clinton years, we'd go to family gatherings and listen to the screeds and the diatribes against the liberals, and sooner or later she and I would make eye contact, and we knew. It was like being on the same radio frequency. We would back each other up whenever an argument was too juicy not to join in, and we would calm each other down when it just wasn't worth creating familial enmity.

I was at her home when she died on Dec. 31. I don't know for sure if she knew I was there, but I'd like to think she could hear my words in her final hours. I tried my best to give her comfort and to let her see me smile, just a little bit. At her bedside, I vowed to myself that I would fight for her, even if I couldn't save her.

The insidious thing about uterine and ovarian cancer is that, unlike breast cancer, it can’t be detected by a lump. In Stephanie's case, they didn't know she had a mass in her abdomen until she finally demanded a full-body scan.

It doesn't have to be like this for other women. Not only do we need more media attention paid to this disease, and of course more money for research into prevention and early detection of uterine and ovarian cancer, but also, women just need to be more aware. They need to talk to their doctors and nurses about those seemingly harmless fibroids, and they need to start demanding that these things be removed, before the real problems begin. My wish is that along with your commitment to address the broken health care system, that you and Mr. Biden also make it a priority to help scientists figure out a way for women to more precisely identify their risk factors based on genetic makeup.

On January 5, I buried my lifelong friend, and the world has one less crazy redhead and brilliant mind to enrich it. And now I plan to spend the rest of my life working toward a future where no other women have to go through what Stephanie went through. I hope that you will remember Stephanie's story and the thousands of others like it.

Stephanie's illness, her death and now her absence still seems so random and improbable, like cancer got the wrong address and decided to stick around long enough to fully break all our hearts.

If illness is not random, and there is some kind of order to the world, then I am not sure I will ever stop being angry at God.

When attempting to drag me to church a few weeks ago, I pointed out to my husband, "In case you hadn't noticed, God and I aren't on speaking terms right now."

Doubt and anger and questioning one's faith feels a little sophomoric at the age of 35. If I have not figured it out by now, what's the point? Stephanie and I come from a long line of stoic Dutch Calvinists. We were tasked with memorizing the densely-annotated catechism in sixth grade. The execution of this task, at least in my case, was not exemplary, but I do remember that the first question and answer explains how most of our people deal with life, and with death. I personally gave up on Calvin and this particular brand of theology a long time ago, but it goes a little something like this:

> What is thy only comfort in life and death? Answer: That I with body and soul, both in life and death, (a) am not my own, (b) but belong unto my faithful Saviour Jesus Christ; (c) who, with his precious blood, has fully satisfied for all my sins, (d) and delivered me from all the power of the devil;

> (e) and so preserves me (f) that without the will of my heavenly Father, not a hair can fall from my head; (g) yea, that all things must be subservient to my salvation, (h) and therefore, by his Holy Spirit, He also assures me of eternal life, (i) and makes me sincerely willing and ready, henceforth, to live unto him. (j)
>
> (Heidelberg Catechism. Lord's Day I, Question 1)

This belief system does not leave a lot of room for a girl to rage against the dying of the light. How could I not rattle heaven's gates with my anger at the dying of a girl who'd just passed the bar, who'd barely been married a year, and with whom I'd delighted in every step of her courtship.

I can still remember when she first spotted our old high school newspaper colleague sitting in the crowd at the Sox game. She called me at my home in Texas, and I could hear the roar of the fans.

"You'll never guess who is sitting two rows ahead of me!"

"Richard Roeper?"

"Nope."

"Steve Guttenburg?"

"What? NO! Where did that come from?"

"I don't know, Steph, why don't you just tell me who is sitting two rows in front of you."

Then she told me.

And then we were two giggling girls back at Illiana Christian High School in Lansing, Illinois. The two had never dated each other in high school, but together they had weathered the investigation of a scandal involving the basketball team, a keg party, cops and a school board cover-up.

Stephanie now found herself wondering whether she should go up and talk to her former co-editor.

"Oh for Pete's sake. Go talk to him. If you don't, you'll always regret it."

The two of them reconnected that night, and started dating almost immediately. He was just as funny as she remembered from high school. After one of their first dates, another couple at the restaurant confessed they had been eavesdropping on Dan and Steph's entire conversation because they were so hilarious together.

In the spring of 2008, just a few short months after getting married, doctors found blood clots in her lungs, and began treating her with blood thinners. Then summer came, and brought with it headaches and vomiting. She had had enough, and she demanded a full body scan, saying, "You need to figure out what's wrong with me, now." That's when they found the tumor on her brain which had metastasized from a mass at her uterus.

Stephanie lost her beautiful, thick red hair, and so much more. She became sad that life was not fun anymore. She grew tired of having to be babysat, though she was so appreciative of her fiercely devoted husband, her mom, her dad, and her amazing sister who, as a teacher, gave up her summer job to be by her side.

Half way through, the doctors thought the chemotherapy treatments were working. Around that time, my husband and I moved to Indiana and I was able to visit Stephanie more frequently, but still not as frequently as I would have liked to, had I known how short our time was going to be.

Stephanie and I had our last shopping trip together in November. She still shopped like a girl who had her whole life ahead of her: buying a coat that would look cute with this outfit, buying a candleholder for the mantle once the Christmas decorations came down.

The day before Thanksgiving, she received the bad news that the chemo was no longer working. The doctors had found another spot on her brain and another one on her spine. On December 12, she got the news that all cancer patients dread the most. There was nothing more that could be done. Steph asked Dan to call me to see if I wanted to come and say goodbye.

In a blind panic, I yanked my poor husband away from his job and we rushed to Northwestern Hospital to see her. When we arrived, she and Dan were calm and conversational. We sat and chatted, along with my dad. She and I watched some ridiculously meta Christmas special that counted down the top 50 all-time greatest moments of American Christmas specials.

Dan mocked me when I made everybody sit reverently quiet during the Bing Crosby/David Bowie duet; Steph laughed as Dan and I discussed the travesty that such a countdown list had left out the Star Wars Christmas Special. I learned for the first time that Stephanie agreed with me about Dean Martin. Not only was he better looking than Frank Sinatra, but invariably more fun to listen to. That was the last real conversation I had with my crazy redhead.

Ever since she was first diagnosed, the extended family would receive weekly updates via e-mail from her mom, my Aunt Bev. These were frequently heartbreaking, sometimes uplifting, but always well-written and full of grace and gratitude. The e-mails that came in after the news of Dec. 12 told me the end was near. Stephanie was slipping away, and mostly she wanted to sit and hold hands with the loved ones around her.

My Stephanie does not hold hands. On December 29 I got a call from Dan that they were putting her in hospice care, but keeping her at home. I was there the next afternoon, kicking myself for not having tried harder to spend more time with her.

I brought along a stack of snapshots that I'd collected over the years, to let her know that this is how I would remember her: her fiendishly cutting into a pizza at Aurelio's Pizzeria. Singing karaoke in cousin Heather's basement. Making doomed gingerbread houses with Kim, Heather and me. The family would use some of these for the photo collage at the visitation and funeral a few days later. I tried my best to give her comfort. I held her hand and patted her arm. I straightened out her wedding ring.

I still have not deleted her number off my speed dial, and I just recently got up the nerve to look at her snapshots that were returned to me after the funeral. I talk about her all the time, not shying away from the fact of her death. She is on my mind often, and I concentrate on how beautiful she was at her wedding. But in the middle of the night, I still see the face that had changed so drastically by the illness overtaking her in those last moments.

I told a friend that losing Stephanie has given me that naked feeling of forgetting my purse. Other days, it feels as if I have lost a leg. The grief is so real, it physically feels different. Nothing feels normal anymore, even now that the funeral is past and we've tried to get on with our lives.

I am a writer, trying to make a living as a writer, and so I write. And because of everything that's happened, I write about Stephanie. It is what I do now. In a way, this is my normal life.

For years, Stephanie has been bugging me to collect all my memories of our childhood and put them together in a book. For years, I have avoided it, instead focusing on fiction and short stories. When she went in for her first round of chemo, I sent her a family essay to read for entertainment, and she loved it so much she begged me to send some more. I churned out only three or four more of them in the weeks that followed. I regret that I failed to complete a collection by the time she was gone.

On the day Stephanie died, Aunt Bev told me Stephanie liked my visits because I made her forget she was sick. That might be the biggest and best compliment I have ever received.

Now when I write, no matter how painful it is, I think of it as a way to heal her. The more I write about our candle-making fiascos, the less time I will spend remembering her illness. A part of me, no doubt the grieving part, thinks this will put the hair back on her head and the shine back into her brown eyes, and I will have little time to rage against the dying of the light.

www.ingramcontent.com/pod-product-compliance
Lightning Source LLC
LaVergne TN
LVHW020642100826
845148LV00012B/2292

* 9 7 8 0 9 8 2 4 4 8 4 0 3 *